THE HUMANITARIAN COMPANION

Try To Praise the Mutilated World

Try to praise the mutilated world.
Remember June's long days,
and wild strawberries, drops of wine, the dew.
The nettles that methodically overgrow
the abandoned homesteads of exiles.
You must praise the mutilated world.
You watched the stylish yachts and ships,
one of them had a long trip ahead of it,
while salty oblivion awaited others.
You've seen the refugees heading nowhere,
You've heard the executioners sing joyfully.
You should praise the mutilated world.
Remember the moments when we were together
in a white room and the curtain fluttered.
Return in thought to the concert where music flared.
You gathered acorns in the park in autumn
and leaves eddied over the earth's scars.
Praise the mutilated world
and the grey feather a thrush lost,
and the gentle light that strays and vanishes
and returns.

ADAM ZAGAJEWSKI

'Try to Praise the Mutilated World' from *Without End: New and Selected Poems* by Adam Zagajewski, translated by Clare Cavanagh. Copyright © 2002 Adam Zagajewski. Translation copyright © Farrar, Straus and Giroux. Reprinted by permission of Farrar, Straus and Giroux, Inc.

THE HUMANITARIAN COMPANION

A Guide for International Aid, Development, and
Human Rights Workers

JOHN H. EHRENREICH

PRACTICAL ACTION
Publishing

Intermediate Technology Publications Ltd
trading as Practical Action Publishing
Schumacher Centre for Technology and Development
Bourton-on-Dunsmore, Rugby,
Warwickshire, CV23 9QZ, UK
www.practicalactionpublishing.org

© John Ehrenreich 2005

First published 2005
Reprinted 2008

ISBN 978 1 85339 601 4

All rights reserved. No part of this publication may be reprinted or reproduced or
utilized in any form or by any electronic, mechanical, or other means, now known
or hereafter invented, including photocopying and recording, or in any
information storage or retrieval system, without the written permission of the
publisher.

A catalogue record for this book is available from the British Library.

Since 1974, Practical Action Publishing has published and disseminated books and
information in support of international development work throughout the world.
Practical Action Publishing (formerly ITDG Publishing) is a trading name of
Intermediate Technology Publications Ltd (Company Reg. No. 1159018), the wholly
owned publishing company of Intermediate Technology Development Group Ltd
(working name Practical Action). Practical Action Publishing trades only in support
of its parent charity objectives and any profits are covenanted back to Practical
Action (Charity Reg. No. 247257, Group VAT Registration No. 880 9924 76).

Typeset by J&L Composition, Filey, North Yorkshire
Printed in India

Contents

Contents

Boxes

Introduction

Humanitarian work comes in many varieties. Staff members of humanitarian aid agencies may work in conflict or post-conflict situations or in the wake of a natural disaster. They may help administer a refugee camp or distribute food and shelter to survivors of catastrophic events, or provide emergency healthcare or psychosocial services or help reunite families. Staff members of development agencies may work on less crisis-driven, longer-term development projects, assisting farmers, small businessmen, or local or national government to develop agricultural, industrial and other business enterprises, educational and healthcare institutions and other underpinnings of economic well-being. Human rights workers may investigate or document human rights abuses, advocate for the survivors of such dreadful events, or assist in setting up 'transitional justice' processes. Other humanitarian workers carry out research programs or gather information needed to plan responses to poverty, oppression or disaster. Some humanitarian workers work on short-term assignments, while others may continue to work on a single assignment for many months or even years.

Humanitarian *workers* also come in many varieties. One major source of differences stems from variation in where the worker comes from. Some are expatriates from North America, Europe or other highly industrialized areas; others are expatriates from less wealthy parts of the world who are working in countries other than their own; and some are 'national' or 'local' staff who are working in their own country – although not always close to the place they call 'home'.

For expatriates, no matter where they come from originally, an assignment represents a relatively sharp break with life 'back home.' Making plans and gathering information before an assignment, learning about a different culture, facing possibly unfamiliar health and safety risks and returning home are important issues. For expatriates who come from developing countries, taking a foreign assignment may mean leaving behind – and, perhaps, eventually returning to – a politically, socially or economically difficult situation.

For national and local staff, there are unique concerns, not least of which are the many distinctions an employer may make between national and expatriate staff with respect to wages and benefits, job security and career opportunities. National staff may also face stresses less common for expatriates. They may need to put effort into taking care of their own families at the same time as they carry out their job and they may need to deal with the effects of their own traumatic experiences during the events that led to the need for humanitarian intervention. For these reasons and others, relationships between expatriates and national staff may be characterized by misunderstandings or tensions.

The writer of this book is a North American. The 'voice' in which I write inevitably reflects this. Some of the material in this book – for example, the sections on issues humanitarian workers may face when they leave home for an assignment in a distant land or when you return home at the end of such an assignment – focuses on problems that are more sharply defined for expatriates than for national staff. Other topics – for example, keeping safe and healthy, managing stress, learning how to work with survivors of traumatic experiences – are relevant for both expatriate and national staff. Even with the latter set of topics, however, the experiences of expatriates on the one hand, national and local staff on the other may diverge. To take one example, the specific kinds of stress faced by national and expatriate staff may not be identical, although they are surely overlapping.

Despite these differences, the perspective of this book is that all humanitarian workers face some common challenges and that many of the broad principles of how to deal with these challenges transcend culture. Whether your assignment takes you far from home or not, and whether you are a human rights worker or an aid worker or on the staff of a development project, you must prepare yourself practically and emotionally for your assignment. You work under conditions that present a variety of potential threats to your safety and to your health. Your work is very stressful. You interact day-in, day-out with people who are themselves the survivors of traumatic events. And, eventually, your assignment comes to an end and you must face the practical and emotional challenges of beginning a new assignment or a new job or returning home. Because of the universality of these challenges, in general if not in all of their specifics, I hope that both expatriates and national and local staff of humanitarian organizations and staff of different kinds of humanitarian enterprises will find ideas and techniques that are useful in this book. Be aware, however, that you may have to adapt them to make them match your own background and experience.

Another source of difference among readers lies in your level of training and experience. Some of you are facing a first assignment; others are veterans of many assignments and long experience. My hope is that this book will be useful throughout your career as a humanitarian worker. The risk in this is that the sheer volume of material and detail may seem overwhelming and unmanageable to beginners, while much in the book will seem obvious and familiar to old hands. The best way to use the book, for both groups, is to skim it to get an idea of the contents, then to pick and choose sections that are relevant to you at the particular phase of your career and of your assignment.

The book is organized to match chronologically the stages of an assignment. Start at the beginning.

Chapter 1 addresses actions you can take before beginning an assignment that will increase the likelihood that your assignment will be productive and successful and that you will maintain a sense of emotional well-being while in the field. It walks you through some of the self-assessment that may help you decide whether humanitarian field work is right for you and helps you understand which of your characteristics, abilities, and skills are potential liabilities in the field and, conversely, which of your characteristics, abilities, and skills are potential strengths. It helps you think through the match between you and your agency and your assignment. It then addresses issues you may face working in a culture different from your own and some of the ethical dilemmas and moral ambiguities you should be prepared for before working in the field. Finally, it walks you through the practicalities – what precautions to take to protect your health when abroad, making basic travel arrangements, and being sure you take with you things you will need.

Many of the topics in this chapter are addressed especially to those facing their first assignment, but even experienced workers may find it a useful exercise to review these topics in light of their experience. Many of the more practical suggestions at the end of the chapter are aimed at expatriates and others whose assignment will take them far from home, but the sections on self-assessment, assessment of the match between you and your agency and assignment, and the ethical and moral dilemmas you may face are equally relevant for national and local staff.

Chapter 2 focuses on safety and security in the field. Staff of humanitarian projects face several sources of danger. First, there are the 'normal' risks and dangers of the local environment. The biggest dangers are usually motor vehicle accidents and street crime. The situations that create the need for humanitarian work, such as wars, refugee crises and famines, create additional risks. Finally, in some conflict and post-conflict situations, staff of humanitarian organizations have become direct targets of violence. The first part of the chapter discusses, in general terms, the risks of work on humanitarian projects of all kinds and some general principles of keeping safe. The remainder of the chapter consists of recommendations addressing specific kinds of risk: risks while traveling, driving, walking or using public transportation; safety issues at home; the threat of personal attack; military risks (including land mines); and risks that especially affect women.

Chapter 3 provides advice for keeping you healthy. In the field you may be exposed to diseases and other health risks you are not accustomed to at home and you may have difficulty finding the kind of medical care you expect at home. Becoming sick is, of course, unpleasant and especially so if you are far from home and loved ones. It also interferes with your ability to carry out your job. This chapter suggests three complementary strategies for staying well: preventing exposure to the viruses, bacteria, parasites and other environmental challenges that lead to illness in the first place; keeping your body strong so that you are less likely to succumb to illness if you are exposed; and acting to keep any illness or injuries you do fall prey to from getting worse. Water and food safety, avoiding insect-borne diseases, HIV/AIDS prevention, malaria prophylaxis, dealing with medical care – which may sometimes be a threat to your health rather than a source of help – and first aid are among the topics treated.

Chapter 4 focuses on managing stress. Stress is inevitable for those doing humanitarian work. Many humanitarian workers dismiss the need to deal with stress. 'If you can't stand the heat, get out of the kitchen,' many workers say. 'The whole point of humanitarian work is that there are people in desperate need and we are here to help them. If we can't put their needs ahead of our own, we are in the wrong business.' The facts speak otherwise.

Although many humanitarian workers withstand the rigors of their work without adverse effects, many others do not. One recent study found that as many as one third of recently returned expatriate staff showed significant signs of emotional distress. Studies of national staff have reported similar findings. Equally important, stress and burnout have an adverse impact on the ability of the humanitarian worker to provide services to recipient groups. Workers suffering from the effects of stress are likely to be less efficient and less effective in carrying out their assigned tanks. They become poor decision makers and they may behave in ways that place themselves or other members of the team at risk, or disrupt the effective functioning of the team.

This chapter provides you with tools to help *manage* stress so that you can continue to do your job well. It addresses, first, the need to anticipate possible sources of stress, second, approaches to reducing the expectable stresses of humanitarian work and, finally, methods of dealing with the stresses that do appear. A worker's spiritual beliefs and practices may play an important role in helping them respond to stress, so one section of the chapter addresses spiritual issues.

Chapter 5 shifts the focus from you to your work. Humanitarian workers work with people who have survived terrible experiences – natural disasters, famines, war, ethnic cleansing, political oppression, terrorist attacks, rape and other individual assaults, becoming a refugee. The emotional state of the survivors of such dreadful events has an enormous effect on their ability to cooperate with relief, recovery and reconstruction efforts. Except for psychosocial workers, most humanitarian worker's assignments are not explicitly focused on helping survivors of catastrophes heal emotionally. However, the policies and programs of humanitarian agencies and the ways in which you as an individual humanitarian worker carry out your tasks may make a major contribution to helping the survivors heal or, at least, to helping the survivors deal better with the emotional wounds they have suffered. Conversely, humanitarian work carried out in ignorance of the emotional impact of disaster can interfere with healing and even 're-traumatize' survivors.

This chapter seeks to help you understand the emotional states that the people humanitarian workers work with are likely to experience. It then suggests some approaches to use when you interview or otherwise seek to gather information from the survivors of a disaster. Finally, it examines how you can structure your day-to-day work with survivors to enhance their ability to heal and, at the same time, enhance your own effectiveness.

Chapter 6 addresses issues you will face at the end of an assignment. 'Going home' sounds simpler than 'going away,' but, for many humanitarian workers, going home is the more difficult journey. Whether you were away on a short-term assignment or for an assignment or assignments lasting years; whether your return represents a temporary withdrawal from field work – for example, to enable your children to have access to appropriate educational opportunities – or a permanent end to your work in the field; and whether the end of an assignment is planned or unexpected – for example, when it follows an involuntary evacuation, you may face some unexpected tests. Just as knowledge of what to expect in the field helps when you are facing a new assignment, knowledge of what to expect when you return home helps you prepare better and experience less stress. This chapter seeks to examine the major components of the journey home, from the practical and logistical to the psychological and spiritual. While many of the sections are aimed at expatriates – and especially at those who have been away on extended assignments – the sections on post-assignment emotional and spiritual readjustment are equally relevant for all humanitarian workers and the sections on reconnecting to family and friends are appropriate for any humanitarian worker whose work has taken them away from home and family.

Finally, at the end of the book, the Resources provide supplementary materials, including a checklist of 'what to do and what to take with you' to use as a guide before leaving for your assignment; a brief first aid manual; guidelines for agencies to follow in managing stress in their staff; sample scripts for relaxation exercises; and references and additional resources, both print and internet, that address issues discussed in the book at greater length.

Acknowledgements

Many experienced humanitarian workers from all over the world contributed to this project. John Fawcett, then of World Vision International and now a freelance consultant on stress and trauma management, human resources management and security preparedness based in Phnom Penh, Cambodia, was the original source of the idea to put this book together. John also co-authored Chapter 6 'Going home.' Jim Guy, Executive Director of the Headington Institute in Pasadena, California, which provides consultation, training and clinical services in support of relief and development personnel worldwide, co-authored the section 'Spiritual resources for humanitarian aid workers' in Chapter 2. Amber Elizabeth Gray, formerly clinical director of the Rocky Mountain Survivors Center in Denver, Colorado, and now a freelance consultant on stress and trauma management for humanitarian workers co-authored Chapter 6 with John Fawcett, co-authored the section on spiritual resources in Chapter 1 with Jim Guy, and made many helpful suggestions about other parts of the text. Mike Wessells of the Christian Children's Fund in Richmond, Virginia, made extensive and enormously helpful comments on the entire text. John Fawcett, Ed Hughes, formerly Security Coordinator, Humanitarian Policy and Practice, at InterAction (the largest alliance of US-based international development and humanitarian non-governmental organizations), Max Glaser, formerly safety and security coordinator for Médécins Sans Frontières – Holland, and Michael O'Neill, Security Director, Save the Children, reviewed the material on safety and security. Dr Ted Lankester, Director of Health Care at InterHealth (a London-based medical charity that specializes in the health needs of those traveling abroad) and Dr Mike Jones, Senior Physician at Edinburgh International Health Centre reviewed the health-related material.

I am deeply indebted to the several people who read and made extensive comments on various other parts of the text. These include Dean Ajdukovic of the University of Zagreb and the Society for Psychological Assistance in Zagreb, Croatia; Deanna Beech of Psychologists for Social Responsibility in Washington, DC; Barbara Lopes Cardozo at the US Centers for Disease Control in Atlanta, Georgia; Lynne Cripe at the US Agency for International Development in Washington, DC; Amy Hudnall at the Institute for Rural Health in Boone, North Carolina; Livia Iskandar at Puhli in Djakarta, Indonesia; Nila Kapor-Stanulovic at the University of Novi Sad in Novi Sad, Yugoslavia; Lisa McKay at the Headington Institute in Pasadena, California; Viola Mukasa, at the Hope for African Children

Acknowledgements

Initiative in Kampala, Uganda; Tineke von Pietersom and Winnifred Simon Huisman at the Antares Foundation (a Dutch foundation that provides support in designing psychosocial systems within humanitarian organizations, training and coaching for managers and staff in stress management, and direct psychosocial support for aid workers after critical incidents and prolonged severe stress) in Amsterdam; Jonathan Potter, Executive Director of People in Aid (the international network of development and humanitarian assistance agencies) in London; and Beth Hudnall Stamm at Idaho State University in Pocatello, Idaho. Sharon McQuaide reviewed the entire manuscript with the expertise of an enormously experienced mental health clinician and the acumen of an excellent editor and provided the love and personal support without which this book could never have happened. I owe all of them a great debt of thanks.

CHAPTER 1
Preparing for a field assignment

Know yourself and what you are getting into
   Assess your motives
   Assess your personality characteristics
   Assess the effects that taking your assignment will have on others
   Assess the organizational support you will have from your agency
   Assess your skills

Create predictability
   Gather information
   Prepare to meet a new culture
   Prepare for ethical dilemmas and moral ambiguities
   Prepare to return home

Some practicalities: what to do and what to take
   Protect your health
   Make basic travel arrangements
   What to take with you

Humanitarian workers have jobs that are both enormously gratifying and filled with difficult challenges, painful choices, and uncomfortable stresses. No matter how resilient you may be, these challenges, choices and stresses can take a toll on you physically and emotionally and can affect your ability to continue to work effectively. This chapter focuses on actions you can take *before* you leave for your assignment that will increase the likelihood that your assignment will be productive and successful and that you will maintain a sense of emotional well-being.

Know yourself and what you are getting into

Before you find yourself in a situation that is not to your liking, some assessment is in order. The more you know about your own motives, personality characteristics and abilities, about the impact your assignment will have on your family and about your agency, the better prepared you will be, first, to decide if this is the right assignment for you and, second, assuming you decide the answer is 'yes,' to face the challenges ahead.

Assess your motives

You need to be strongly motivated to choose a difficult path such as humanitarian aid work or human rights work in the field. Why do *you* want to be a humanitarian worker – either in general or in the particular assignment you are about to begin? Different people have different motivations:

- a desire to help others
- a desire to 'make a difference'
- a desire to use your talents
- a desire to do something valuable with your life
- a religious vocation
- a desire to improve your skills and build a career
- a wish for adventure
- a desire to travel
- a need for money
- a wish for time away from home.

No single motivational factor is the 'correct' one to have, but some motivations may be more helpful in maintaining your commitment to humanitarian work than others. Your desire for travel to a warm climate may not suffice to keep you going in difficult and dangerous living conditions. And if your desire to help others is based on a need to feel wanted, experiencing ingratitude from some of the people you try to help may come as a shock. Thinking through what *you* want to get out of an assignment before you go may arm you against later surprises.

Assess your personality

Many different kinds of people work in humanitarian aid, human rights and development projects. There is no one personality type that is perfect for every situation. Some of the characteristics of people who are successful in maintaining their commitment and emotional well-being in field situations include the following.

- Perseverance, patience and a high toleration for frustration.
- A strong sense of responsibility.
- Good communication skills, including an ability to listen effectively, state your own opinions and needs clearly and express your feelings appropriately.

- The ability to work with others on a team: to be assertive yet to cooperate and make compromises when needed and to be able to admit mistakes when it is appropriate.

- The ability to solve problems and make decisions effectively. A good decision maker is thorough and open to considering alternatives, but able to make quick and firm decisions when necessary.

- A sense of adventure, an ability to get pleasure from a wide range of experience and to welcome change.

- Flexibility and resilience in the face of difficult working and living conditions, uncertainty, discomfort and sometimes danger.

- High tolerance for personal diversity, including tolerance for a range of habits, styles of communication, customs, religions, beliefs and cultures.

- Understanding the power of ethnic, religious and national identity and respecting the sensitivities of those whose identify differs from your own.

- Sensitivity to and respect for the distinct experiences and needs that reflect gender differences.

- The ability to relax.

- Empathy, caring and an ability to express and demonstrate support for colleagues and clients, coupled with an ability to maintain an appropriate sense of professional boundaries.

- A sense of being grounded in spiritual or ethical/philosophical beliefs. But consider: Do your beliefs create potential issues of conscience that would make it difficult to work in the situation you face (for example, corruption, working with people who may have participated in atrocities, working with people whose beliefs about violence or about gender or about religious tolerance are very different from yours)?

- A history of having been able to resolve major stressors and traumatic experiences, whether in personal life or in past experiences of humanitarian work.

- A sense of humor, used in a socially and culturally sensitive manner.

To help you think about your own characteristics, you might want to complete the following questionnaire.

Box 1 Temperament and personality checklist

For each item below, circle the number that indicates whether the statement is (1) Not At All True, (2) Just a Little True, (3) Pretty Much True, or (4) Very Much True of you. 'Not at All' means that the behavior is seldom or never true of you, 'Very Much' means that the item is very often or almost always true of you. 'Just a Little' and 'Pretty Much' are in between. Be sure to respond to all items.

		Not at All True	Just a Little True	Pretty Much True	Very Much True
1	I persevere when I don't initially succeed ...	1	2	3	4
2	I am patient when I can't accomplish a task immediately ...	1	2	3	4
3	I have a high toleration for frustration ...	1	2	3	4
4	I have an 'even' temperament (I am not very moody; I don't have a lot of big mood swings) ...	1	2	3	4
5	I am optimistic ...	1	2	3	4
6	I have a strong sense of responsibility for my actions ...	1	2	3	4
7	I am a good listener ...	1	2	3	4
8	When I speak, I can express my ideas easily ...	1	2	3	4
9	I like working as part of a team ...	1	2	3	4
10	I can admit my own mistakes ...	1	2	3	4
11	I am comfortable asserting my own beliefs, but I can compromise when it is appropriate ...	1	2	3	4
12	I am confident about my ability to solve problems ...	1	2	3	4
13	I make decisions easily ...	1	2	3	4
14	Other people see me as having good common sense ...	1	2	3	4
15	I have good judgment about people ...	1	2	3	4
16	I am good at judging whether a situation is dangerous ...	1	2	3	4
17	I have a sense of adventure ...	1	2	3	4
18	I get pleasure from a wide range of experience ...	1	2	3	4
19	I welcome change ...	1	2	3	4

cont.

Box 1 *continued*

		1	2	3	4
20	I don't get flustered when I am faced with an unexpected change in plans or an unexpected situations ...	1	2	3	4
21	I am able to tolerate difficult living conditions ...	1	2	3	4
22	I am able to tolerate difficult working conditions ...	1	2	3	4
23	Uncertainty doesn't bother me ...	1	2	3	4
24	I can tolerate a degree of danger ...	1	2	3	4
25	I enjoy being with people whose customs and culture are different from my own ...	1	2	3	4
26	I am comfortable with people whose religion and value systems are different from mine ...	1	2	3	4
27	I am comfortable working with people who do not share my own political beliefs ...	1	2	3	4
28	I respect how sensitive people are about their ethnic, religious and national identity ...	1	2	3	4
29	I recognize how different the experiences of men and women can be ...	1	2	3	4
30	I can relax easily ...	1	2	3	4
31	I am not usually a worrier ...	1	2	3	4
32	I readily understand other people's feelings, thoughts and motives ...	1	2	3	4
33	I am supportive towards colleagues ...	1	2	3	4
34	I can keep my professional relationships (for example, with clients) separate from my personal ones ...	1	2	3	4
35	I find continued meaning and purpose in life ...	1	2	3	4
36	I have a strong sense of spirituality ...	1	2	3	4
37	I have a good sense of humor ...	1	2	3	4

Scoring: Add up your score.

37–95   Are you sure a field assignment is right for you?
96–110   You are probably okay, but think carefully about your vulnerabilities
111–148 You clearly have the characteristics typical of people who are successful in field situations.

Regardless of your total score, think carefully about any items on which you gave yourself a '1' or a '2'. These are characteristics that could give you trouble. Be aware of them and try to compensate for them.

Assess the effects that taking your assignment will have on others

Taking on an assignment affects not only you, but your family, friends and colleagues. In turn, their reactions will have an impact on your own sense of well-being.

If your family will be accompanying you, what effect will your taking on this assignment have on them? What will your spouse or partner be doing? What will the effect be on your children of being uprooted and transported to a culture that is foreign to them? What practical issues will arise with respect to schooling, healthcare and safety?

If your assignment will take you away from your family and close friends, what practical and emotional problems will your absence create for them? How will they feel about your absence? How will they cope with these problems and feelings? If your assignment will take you into potentially risky situations, what is your family's level of toleration of risk, as well as your own?

If you are taking a leave from your regular job, what effect will your absence have on your colleagues and on your career? At the most practical level, can you maintain your benefits, such as health insurance or life insurance or pension rights? Will your job still be waiting for you when you return? Beyond these, what will the impact be on your colleagues? Will your experience on your assignment or your absence affect your long term career goals?

Assess the organizational support you will have from your agency

While you are in the field, your work team and your agency assume the role of your family, your friends and your job, all rolled into one. They are, potentially, your strongest base of support, but they can also be a source of strain or of disappointment. Before you embark on an assignment, you want to be sure there is a good 'fit' between you and your agency. (Note that, in many cases, you will not be able to get good answers to these questions before you go to the field. A certain toleration for ambiguity and uncertainty is needed for working in the field.)

- Are the aims, mission, and immediate goals of the agency acceptable to you? Where do these goals come from? Assessments of need? Consultation with potential recipients of aid? Donor concerns? Political or media concerns?

- Are you going to be comfortable with the working methods the agency uses? What does the agency realistically expect you to accomplish?

- Are you comfortable with the work load the agency will demand of you?

- Does the practical support your agency provides for staff meet your needs and expectations? Does the agency have the funds, staffing and other resources to do the job it is asking you to do? Does it have policies in place to protect its employees' health, safety and well-being? (More on this can be found under Resources at the end of this book).

- Do you feel comfortable with any expectations the agency has regarding your religious beliefs or practices?

- Does the emotional support your agency provides for staff meet your needs and expectations? What is the 'culture' of the agency like? Is it one of mutuality or of hierarchy? Of supportiveness or of assigning blame? Is it informal or formal and bureaucratic? Does it recognize good work?

- What kind of people will you be working with, on a day-to-day basis?

- Does your organization adhere to the codes of good practices and standards of behavior that the international humanitarian aid community has increasingly agreed to.

Over the past decade, three major sets of standards have been developed. These are the *Recommendations for an Accountable Organization* prepared by the Humanitarian Accountability Project – an initiative of the British Red Cross Society, CARE International, Caritas Internationalis, The Danish Agency for Development Assistance, International Rescue Committee, the Norwegian Refugee Council, Oxfam GB, and several other NGOs; the *Private Voluntary Organization Standards* prepared by InterAction – the largest alliance of US-based international development and humanitarian non-governmental organizations, with more than 160 member organizations operating in every developing country; and the *Code of Good Practice in the management and support of aid personnel* prepared by People in Aid – a London-based network of more than 50 development and humanitarian assistance agencies based all over the world.

The standards are too lengthy to reproduce in full in this manual, but they are readily accessed via the internet (see Resources for more details). You should enquire whether your agency adheres to these standards. If it does not, a reading of the standards will suggest specific questions you should ask of your agency and the answers you have a right to expect. In asking these questions, note that agencies come in various sizes and have various missions. While many agencies might aspire to provide all of the support and employment conditions listed in the standards and codes, they do not all achieve them fully. Expectations need to be realistic.

Assess your skills

Do you have the skills you need to carry out your assignment? Can you adapt your technical skills to the task requirements? Before you find yourself in the middle of a task that you do not have the know-how to do, you might seek out the training you need. This may include not only training in skills directly related to your assignment, but learning the language of the country to which you are going, taking a first aid course, or taking a safety and security training program.

The novice humanitarian worker should be aware that humanitarian work will place many unexpected demands on you. Although you may expect simply to ply your trade as engineer, health worker, teacher, or other outside expert, you may also be called on to play a management role to which you are not accustomed. For example, you may have to become involved in activities such as selecting suitable personnel, supervising other staff, finding office space and setting up an office, setting up a vehicle maintenance program, budgeting, setting up and maintaining bookkeeping and other record keeping systems, and fundraising. Taking on a management role may be relatively straightforward or may be complicated by cross-cultural issues. For example, a young female staff member may be asked to manage older men in a society by whose traditions this represents an abnormal cultural situation.

You need to be prepared for this and to be prepared to acquire the new skills you will need to do it well. References to several books addressing this topic can be found in the Resources. If you would prefer more formal training, courses in 'NGO management' or 'Management of non-profit organizations' are offered by many universities. Look for these courses in university-level schools of business or schools of public health, or look for programs in 'peace studies.' An internet search can find one near you.

Create predictability

The more you know about what to expect when you are in the field, the less anxious you will be and the better prepared you will be to deal with the challenges of your assignment once you get there. Gather information about your agency, assignment and specific job. Learn about the culture you will be entering. Think about the deeper implications of an outsider providing 'help.' The following sections discuss each of these themes in more detail.

Gather information

Your agency should provide you with a thorough orientation before you leave for your assignment. This should provide information about:

- The agency's mission and structure.

- The history and context of the specific disaster, emergency, incident or crisis in which you will be working.

- The history of your agency's involvement in the country and region and its reputation.

- The specific project and your job description.

- The resources you will have to carry out your work, such as transport, facilities, equipment and budget.

- Terms of employment. Be sure to check:
    - Salary: How much will you be paid? When and how?
    - What expenses will you be reimbursed for? When and how?
    - Benefits, including health insurance, life insurance, pensions, etc.
    - Accommodation and food in the field

- Expectations regarding workload, hours, time off for rest and recreation, vacations
- Policies with respect to practical, financial and legal support if needed as a result of job-related events.

■ Safety and security policies and practices – including evacuation policies and plans. The orientation should give you a realistic sense of the level of danger involved in the project, so that you can make an informed decision as to whether it is the right project for you.

■ Specific travel plans, including who will meet you on arrival or where you should go, as well as details of initial living accommodation.

Unfortunately, many organizations provide staff with only a minimal orientation before the staff member leaves, often assuring the staff member that they will get the information they need once they arrive at their assignment. That puts the burden on you to find out as much as you can before you leave on your own. You should feel free to ask questions of human resources staff and the person in the home office who is in charge of your project. You may also want to be put in contact with staff who have recently returned from the project or who are currently in the field. If you feel there is reluctance to provide you with the kind of information listed above, ask a hard 'why'?

Supplement what the agency provides with your own investigations as to what to expect. Talk to people who have recently returned – from the country or region, if it is not possible to find someone from the specific site. Use the library or the internet to gather information about the country, the culture and the political/social context in which you will be working. Several internet sources may also provide current, if general, information on the security situation (see Resources). Be aware that you may be told some 'scare stories,' but also be aware that some of these stories may be true.

Read this manual thoroughly. It will provide you with at least the basics of what you need to know about safety and security, physical health, self-care, managing stress, working with survivors of traumatic events, as well as issues related to ending your assignment and a list of further resources if you want to learn more.

Prepare to meet a new culture

When you first arrive in a new culture, you are likely to be excited by the novelty. But often, after a while, the excitement wears off. The lack of familiarity may begin to grate on you. Unnecessary hassles and inefficiency you do noy expect at home may produce feelings of irritation and annoyance. You may miss the conveniences and comforts of home and may become judgmental about the culture of your host country.

Culture shock as this is sometimes called, can produce a lack of interest in the other culture: some people find themselves trying to spend time with compatriots and avoiding local people. Others may find themselves responding to the host culture with feelings of superiority. Still others may over-compensate by over-identifying with the host culture and becoming overly ready to abandon their own culture. Over time, if you stick it out, you usually adapt. The local culture will come to feel more familiar and you will become more able to appreciate many aspects of the local culture and to cope with those you still find disturbing.

If you will be working in a country or region you are not already familiar with, you should try to learn as much as possible about its customs, life style, language, food and culture before you go, in order to reduce potential culture shock. Read books about the country you are going to. Find out about it on the internet. See films made in the country or set in the country. Take a language course or a course at a local university in the culture of the region. Seek out people from the country you are going to who live in your own area. Adjust your expectations: be prepared for a pace of life or attitudes about time or work or customs that are unfamiliar and which, in your own culture, may be undesirable.

One set of cross-cultural issues that can trip you up reflects the enormous variation around the world in patterns of belief and behavior. We are normally barely conscious of our own cultural expectations about such issues as the appropriate way to greet people and answer questions, what to wear, how to deal with the opposite sex and how to express feelings, yet violations of them are very jarring. Imagine if someone you are talking to you stands too close to you (or, depending on your culture, too far away). It is jarring and pushes us away. Some behaviors that unwittingly violate cultural expectations may be very offensive. Learning about some of these expectations lessens the likelihood that you will behave in ways that cause offense to the local people you will be working with. More positively, demonstrating respect for local people and treating them with dignity contributes to their psychosocial well-being.

Learning all these unspoken rules may seem overwhelming. An internet search – try searching, for example, under 'etiquette' and the name of the country – e.g., 'etiquette in Kenya' – may be helpful. But beware: many of the published books and articles on etiquette are geared to businessmen doing business in that country and may not fully reflect the practices of less affluent people.

Remember, too, that people in the local culture recognize that you are foreign. Local people are likely to recognize that foreigners are a bit 'odd' and they may understand that a different set of rules applies when dealing with an outsider than when dealing with others from the same culture. Asking about local expectations is likely to be seen as a sign of respect. Local people will not be offended if a foreigner does not know all the nuances of their customs, but are likely to become offended and consider the foreigner arrogant if he or she does not try to learn appropriate behaviors after having lived in the country.

Differences across cultures are not confined to relatively simple rules of everyday behavior. One set of possible differences concerns gender roles. Women from western countries may face a very different role and status for women in some of the countries in which they work. For women (and men) who come from societies

Box 2   Cross-cultural issues

- What are the conventional rules of politeness and decency? How do you greet a stranger the first time you meet him or her? What about an acquaintance? Do you shake hands, embrace, or 'air kiss' both cheeks?

- What are the rules of body language? How far do people stand from one another when talking? Do they make eye contact? What gestures are considered rude?

- What is the dress code? Are bared arms (for example, short sleeves) or bared legs (for example, shorts or a short skirt) considered improper, in either men or women?

- How do you engage in conversations that have a specific goal or purpose (for example, a business arrangement)? Do you come 'straight to the point' or are extended social niceties expected first? Are questions about the family or health of a person you do not know well expected, or inappropriate?

- What are the assumptions about cross-gender behavior? Is it appropriate for a man to talk with a strange woman other than in the company of her husband? Is it appropriate to shake hands with someone of the opposite gender? What constitutes the appropriate respect to people of either gender? And what is considered disrespectful?

- What are the assumptions about treatment of elders? Are there distinct ways of greeting someone older than you and someone younger?

- What are local attitudes towards time? Is punctuality expected?

- Do individuals make decisions on their own, or only after consultation with associates or their family? Does the husband make decisions for the whole family?

- What emotions is it appropriate to express in public? How are they expressed?

- How do you call for attention in a store or a restaurant or in a government office? Is waiting in line expected?

- How do you express disagreement? Is it expressed openly? Is frankness valued more than saving face, or vice versa?

- Are there particular cultural blunders to avoid, such as eating with the left hand or failing to remove your shoes before entering a home?

in which roles for professional women have expanded dramatically in the past thirty years and in which professional women are very visible and respected, working in a culture in which such roles are all but unknown for women and in which women are invisible or silenced or seen as 'lesser' presents both a cultural shock and a variety of practical obstacles to effective work. Discussion with other women about the obstacles they have faced and strategies they have followed for dealing with them can help prepare you for this. Differences in expectations regarding appropriate behavior by men and women can lead to major, and sometimes potentially dangerous, misunderstandings. See the discussion on sexual harassment, in Chapter 2.

Cross-cultural differences in attitudes towards sexual orientation are also a potential source of serious misunderstanding. In the industrialized countries of North America, western Europe and Australia and New Zealand, attitudes towards homosexuality have become relatively relaxed in recent years. In some parts of the world, however, open expression of homosexuality remains a major violation not only of cultural taboos but of the law. Criminal penalties can be very severe – up to the death penalty. Gay or lesbian workers need to be aware of this and regulate their behavior accordingly.

Another 'cross-cultural' issue to be aware of are the usually unspoken differences in power between humanitarian workers and the people they seek to help. Most obviously, expatriate workers have far greater wealth and far greater access to those with power than most of the people they are working with. The aid worker can also leave, more or less at will, while the recipients of assistance are tied to the aid location. At a deeper level, many of what are now the poorer countries of the world were, not very long ago, colonies or dependencies of the same countries that now are sending humanitarian assistance. Even now they remain in an economically dependent relationship. Europeans and North Americans, even those whose home country did not directly colonize the site of their humanitarian work, may share skin color and certainly share culture with people from the country that did. From the perspective of the recipients of assistance, long histories of disempowerment and heavily inculcated feelings of cultural inferiority and expectations of deference and dependency complicate any relationships, however superficially benign, with those from outside.

The same issues may characterize the relations between expatriate humanitarian workers and national staff. The expatriate is a guest in the receiving culture, but often plays the role of a dominant guest, who insists that his or her own efficiency and interaction rules must be followed within the work group. Expatriates are usually paid far better, have more job security, and have a clearer career path both within their agency and in the humanitarian enterprise as a whole. The expatriate will eventually leave; the national staff member will remain behind, often without the financial support of the currently employing agency. Unlike most expatriates, national staff may have experienced many of the same traumatic experiences and share political and cultural allegiances with those they seek to help. Feelings of identification with, or embarrassment about, local culture may appear. The experiences of humanitarian staff who are natives of other less economically developed areas but have been seconded intra-agency to another country are, in some respects, intermediate between those of European and North American expatriates and local staff. Issues such as salary (should it stay on the local scale or be on the same scale as the consultants from outside the region?), home leave and feelings about having abandoned one's own, often very needy, situation and people may loom large.

There are no simple formulas for dealing with these issues of power, but an awareness of them – for both expatriates and national staff – and a self-conscious effort to base interactions on humility, mutual respect, transparency and true partnership is a good starting point.

Prepare for ethical dilemmas and moral ambiguities

Whatever your own individual motives for working in a humanitarian aid, human rights, or development project, virtually all humanitarian workers want to 'make a difference' and want to 'help other people.' But in the real world of humanitarian work, it is not always entirely clear what helps people and what actions, though intended to help people, may actually harm them. Humanitarian agencies and their staff inescapably, though usually tacitly, carry and wield power. Their actions have consequences and the intended positive effects of these actions are inevitably and inextricably mixed with less positive ones.

Forewarned is forearmed. There are no easy answers to the dilemmas discussed below, but it is helpful to know ahead of time that they exist, to think about your own reactions to them and to find out how your agency deals with them. The Red Cross has described the obligation to give humanitarian assistance wherever it is needed and the converse belief that those in desperate need have a human *right* to be helped as the *humanitarian imperative*. To make it possible to fulfill the humanitarian imperative, humanitarian organizations traditionally insisted on three principles to govern their actions:

- *Impartiality*: Aid should be offered solely on need and should not be dependent on factors such as the nationality, race, class, ethnicity, religion or political opinions of recipients.

- *Neutrality*: Humanitarian agencies have an obligation to refrain from taking sides in conflicts or engaging in controversies of a political, racial, religious, or ideological nature. They should not act in ways that assist, or hamper, one side to the exclusion of the other.

- *Independence*: Humanitarian organizations should be independent of governmental, political, religious or other extraneous affiliations.

Only by adhering to these rules, it was argued, could humanitarian organizations create the *humanitarian space*, divorced from conflict and political interference, that permits humanitarian assistance to take place. The Red Cross 'Code of Conduct,' the 'Humanitarian Charter and Minimum Standards in Disaster Response' prepared by the Sphere Project, and the *Private Voluntary Organization Standards* prepared by InterAction describe, at varying levels of specificity, how humanitarian agencies should act to comply with these standards. These documents can be readily accessed through the Internet (see Resources).

But in the real world of complex humanitarian emergencies, it may not be possible to provide humanitarian assistance at all unless you are willing to take actions that violate one or other of the principles. In other situations, one of these principles may directly conflict with another or may conflict with other humanitarian values and goals, such as supporting human rights, promoting peace or encouraging socioeconomic development. When conflicts arise among various principles and between acting on these principles and acting in the best interests of recipients, various humanitarian agencies respond in different ways, depending on their structure, organizational philosophies and particular missions. Individual humanitarian workers, too, may be placed in the situation of having to balance competing values and principles.

Independence and impartiality

Without resources, your agency cannot give aid at all. However, donors – especially governmental donors – may not give money with no strings attached. The aid agency's priorities, in part at least, must accord with the priorities of the donors, not the needs of potential recipients.

Some of the most intense dilemmas this creates arise when aid is given in the context of military occupation – for example, in Iraq in the months after the war to overthrow Saddam Hussein, or in countries such as Bosnia or Liberia in which there are international peace-keeping forces. The independent goals of the aid agency become blurred. Is it possible to provide completely disinterested aid, or will aid, whatever its intentions, inevitably be seen as an effort to 'win the hearts and minds' of the local people in support of the military operation?

What if the agency or its staff disapproves of the military's priorities or even of the entire military presence? Must it withdraw, violating the humanitarian imperative? If it does not, does accepting financial support from a government whose military forces are occupying the country, or logistical support from the military itself, distort the priorities of the agency? The military may be efficient at flying in supplies and providing logistical support, but it may be less interested in traditional values of humanitarian agencies such as local empowerment, community building, strengthening families and sensitivity to local culture. If, despite such concerns, the aid agency cooperates with the military, it may create a perception, if not a reality, that the aid agency is an arm of the military. That, in turn, ties the moral legitimacy of the aid mission to the perceived moral legitimacy of the occupation. It may also expose aid agency staff to attack from forces the military is suppressing.

Potential violations of the principle of neutrality may also arise for staff of agencies with religious affiliations. It is hard for staff affiliated with a faith-based agency not to be seen by recipients as *missionaries*, no matter how neutral the agency tries to be in its actual work. Your mere presence and all of your actions are inevitably perceived as *statements* about your values. Even secular agencies may be seen as implicitly promoting *Western* or *secular* values.

Neutrality

Complex humanitarian emergencies have a moral complexity. They are created or intensified by human actions – for example, political repression, international or civil war, ethnic cleansing, clashes of economic interests. Even the effects of natural disasters may be exacerbated by past or current governmental policies. A complete adherence to the principle of neutrality would require aid agencies to limit their response to the consequences of the disaster and to ignore the underlying causes. This may be an uncomfortable position. You may feel one side or the other in a conflict is more deserving of blame.

In fact, the goal of *neutrality* may be a hopeless illusion. In most circumstances, treating both parties to a conflict *equally* in fact benefits one at the expense of the other. For example, if one side to a conflict is well endowed with arms, an arms embargo applied equally to both sides – as it was in Bosnia – mainly hurts the side with fewer arms. For another example, a refugee camp on the border, intended to help civilian victims of a conflict, may provide a protected haven for combatants. (This happened, for example, in Rwanda). Even when aid benefits both sides equally, it may prolong the conflict. For instance, food aid may be exchanged for guns or control over the distribution of food in a refugee camp may be used by one faction among the refugees to control other factions.

Sometimes, an agency's actions may undermine its neutrality, if not objectively, then in the eyes of local people. For instance, in many contexts, an agency can only carry out activities in a war zone with government permission, which, if obtained, taints the agency and its employees in the eyes of the government's adversaries. Other, similar dilemmas may arise with respect to local militias (both state-sanctioned and unsanctioned), warlords, tribal chiefs and their equivalents.

Human rights

Human rights agencies and agencies providing humanitarian aid or operating economic development projects, despite sharing many values, may have conflicting interests in practice. Providing humanitarian assistance or running a development project requires gaining the assent if not the cooperation of local and national authorities, but those very authorities may be persistent violators of the human rights of the population the humanitarian agency seeks to help. If the agency and its staff are to provide aid, they may be inhibited from revealing what they know about human rights abuses committed by the authorities. Among other things, the need for access may expose the aid agency to extortion: For example, it may only be able to provide aid if it pays local warlords to provide security services, or if it permits them to tax the incomes of national staff. Dealing with morally or financially corrupt authorities provides the latter with a facade of legitimacy, which may help them consolidate their power.

Another possible conflict between human rights and humanitarian agencies is that the human rights agency seeks justice for the victims of abuses, while, to relieve material suffering, the aid agency promotes peace. But in the short run, at least, seeking justice may embitter those brought to justice and intensify a cycle of revenge.

Doing no harm

Even in situations in which there is no ongoing conflict, providing aid may unintentionally harm the recipients. Consider several examples.

1 An agency distributes food. This may inhibit long term socioeconomic development by undermining the prices of locally produced commodities. Yet if the aid agency were to shift to a 'development-oriented' strategy, it may be too slow to respond to emergency situations – for example, a drought-induced famine.

2 An aid agency legitimately seeks to identify and strengthen local leadership. But who are chosen to be leaders and how? Do the leaders whose power is supported by their relationship with the aid agency represent the unjust status quo that led to conflict in the first place? Do the leaders chosen help maintain a family and community structure that is deeply oppressive of women? Or, conversely, do they seek to change the old ways in a fashion that promotes new conflicts in the society?

3 An aid agency ends up providing not just emergency help but long-term assistance. The agency's provision of medicines, health services, education and training and food may legitimize and support a government which has abandoned its people.

4 The government of the country where aid is given has a policy that you believe is clearly unjust – for example, refusing to educate women. Does your agency suspend aid to try to force the government to change its policies – violating the humanitarian imperative – or does it continue aid, even though this helps stabilize the government and makes the overall situation less tolerable for many people, including at least some women.

Prepare to return home

It may seem strange to talk about preparing to come home when you have not even left yet, but you are probably used to doing this when you take a minor trip. For instance, when you leave for a vacation, you arrange to have the mail held and the dog walked, so that you do not face an untidy situation when you return. Going away for a lengthier period creates more significant challenges for your return.

For many humanitarian workers, going home is more difficult than going away. Whether your return represents a temporary withdrawal from field work – for example, to enable your children to have access to appropriate educational opportunities – or a permanent end to your work in the field, and whether the end to your assignment is unexpected – for example, when it follows an involuntary evacuation – or is long planned, a variety of issues are likely to appear. We will discuss these issues and suggest how to handle them in detail in Chapter 6, but the day you buy your ticket home is too late to start preparing. Some of the suggestions made in Chapter 6 require you to start to act before you leave and continue acting while you are away.

Skim Chapter 6 before you leave. Some of the suggestions you may want to act on include the following:

- If you work in a licensed profession – for example, in the USA, medicine, nursing, social work – check what you will have to do to maintain your license while you are away.

- Plan to get letters of reference from each of your supervisors and employers in the field while you are still in the field. Get copies of your job descriptions and save them. You may also need to get police clearances. All of these will be difficult, if not impossible to get after you return.

- If you are away for an extended period, it is easy to get 'out of touch' with your home culture. This can make re-entry unnecessarily difficult. Plan ways of keeping up with your home culture while you are away. You might subscribe to a local news or sports or cultural magazine or regularly read an internet version of a local newspaper.

- Even more important, plan ways of keeping in touch with your family and friends. Maintain regular communication with people back home who can keep you up to date. Ask someone back home to hold on to copies of your letters and e-mails so that you can trace your own development when you return.

- Expect that you will change, your family will change and your home country will change, while you are away.

Some practicalities: what to do and what to take

Before you leave for your assignment, be sure to do the following. A 'Before You Go' checklist, to help you make sure you have not forgotten anything, can be found in Resources.

Protect your health

See your doctor

You will need to arrange for any necessary immunizations, malaria prophylaxis if appropriate, and obtain copies of prescriptions for medications you take on an ongoing basis. Give yourself plenty of lead time: Some immunizations require several booster shots at several week intervals and some types of malaria prophylaxis must be started several weeks before you leave.

You do not usually need a general physical if you will be on assignment for only a short time, but it is a good idea in any of the following situations:

1 you have not had a checkup in over a year

2 your assignment will be in a relatively remote area with little access to medical care

3 you will be going on an extended assignment (six months or more)

4 you are pregnant or nursing or you have a pre-existing medical condition that might be affected by travel or that raises special issues for travelers. Examples include diabetes, epilepsy, heart, liver, or kidney problems, skin conditions, history of splenectomy, compromised immune system function

5 you are age 50 or over.

While you are with the doctor, find out your blood type and any sensitivities to medications (including anti-malarials) you may have.

See your dentist
See your dentist, well in advance of your departure. Have a thorough dental check and have any dental work you need done before you leave. Dental care in many parts of the world may be unreliable; anesthetics may not be available; and any procedure in which blood flows carries a risk of HIV or Hepatitis B infection.

Obtain necessary immunizations
Consult your doctor or a travel medicine clinic for the appropriate shots for the areas to which you will be going. Diphtheria/tetanus, Hepatitis A, and Typhoid shots are needed no matter where you are going, and Hepatitis B shots are almost always needed if you are going to the developing world. Depending on where you are going and how long you are staying, you may also need immunization against yellow fever (you will also need an international certificate of immunization against yellow fever for entry to many countries), Meningitis, Japanese Encephalitis, and/or Rabies. Polio shots are still needed in some areas. Measles, tick-born encephalitis, influenza, and pneumococcal pneumonia vaccines are occasionally needed.

Note that some of these immunizations require several shots, so give yourself enough time. And remember that, even if you have previously been immunized, you may be due for a booster: current guidelines call for re-immunization every three years for Japanese Encephalitis, Meningitis, Typhoid, and Rabies; every ten years for the others. An immunity check two to four months after the end of your initial series of Hepatitis B shots will determine if you have achieved long term immunity. If so, no revaccination is needed for at least 15 years, for non-immunocompromised persons.

Begin malaria prophylaxis
Begin malaria prophylaxis, if you are going to an area where malaria is common. There is clear evidence that it is effective. You may need to start taking the pills two to three weeks before leaving, depending on which drug you use. Note that

strains of malaria that are resistant to particular prophylactic regimens are found in many countries, and that the patterns of resistance are constantly changing. Which anti-malarial medication to use depends on where you are going. It is essential to get current advice. Consult your doctor or a tropical medicine clinic.

Get basic training in first aid

Get basic training in first aid, or at least obtain a good first aid manual and familiarize yourself with the basic principles of first aid. There are many good manuals available, in book stores and on-line (see Resources for some suggestions).

Obtain any medical and related supplies you may need

It may be problematic to obtain these once you are on assignment. Your medical supplies should include:

- A supply of any prescription medications you take on a regular basis. If you try to get them away from home, they may not be available at all or may be of questionable quality or out of date. Ask your doctor for a copy of all prescriptions, though, just in case.

- An appropriate antibiotic to be used in case of severe diarrhea, urinary tract infection, skin or ear infections. Take a supply with you. You will need to ask your doctor for a recommendation and appropriate prescription.

- A supply of any over the counter medications you may want. Take medications for allergies, cramps, headaches, diarrhea and athlete's foot.

- A first aid kit. Basic first aid supplies such as antiseptic wipes, antibiotic cream, bandages of various sizes, sterile gauze, adhesive tape, forceps, scissors, latex gloves and oral rehydration tablets. Assemble it yourself or buy a simple kit.

- Sunscreen and a hat with a visor or brim for sun protection. The sunscreen should have an SPF (sun protection factor) of 30. Higher SPFs provide little additional protection, lower not enough. Be sure the lotion provides protection against both UV-A and UV-B rays.

- Insect repellent. The most effective ones contain 25–30 per cent diethyl toluamide (DEET). Higher concentrations of DEET may last longer but are generally unnecessary and may cause local irritation. (Note: For young children, use concentrations of DEET of about 10 per cent; do not use DEET at all on infants under a year of age).

- A spare pair of glasses or contact lenses and a copy of your prescription.

- Personal hygiene items, such as tampons, and condoms and other contraceptives – unless you expect to rigidly abstain from casual sexual encounters.

- Water purification tablets or a small water purification kit.

In addition:

- If you are going to an area where malaria or other flying insect–borne diseases are common, find out if an appropriate mosquito net is provided or is readily available locally. If there is any doubt, take one. Make sure the net is presoaked in permethrin or deltamethrin or lambdacyhalthrin, insecticides that kill mosquitoes. The net will need to be resoaked every six months and whenever it is washed, so also take along an adequate supply of the insecticide for resoaking it. Be sure the net will be big enough to fit loosely enough around your bed so that you will not be pressing your arms or legs against it in the night. It should also be long enough to completely drape on the floor. If it does not, you can tuck it under the mattress, but that increases the risk of a mosquito biting through the net.

- If you will be in an area where there is a high rate of malaria, add a sterile lancet for obtaining a malaria smear. If you will be in an area where reliable medications may be hard to get, take an emergency self-treatment kit. Get specialist advice about this, since resistant strains of the microorganism that causes malaria are common in many areas. Note: In many areas, the organisms that cause malaria are resistant to sufadoxine/pyrmethamine (Fansidar), and use of Fansidar is no longer recommended.

- If you will be stationed in or traveling for anything other than a short visit to an area where there is a high rate of HIV/AIDS, Hepatitis B or Hepatitis C, take a needle and syringe kit. Be sure to get a medical prescription or signed doctor's note stating that these supplies are for your personal medical use only.

- If you will be traveling extensively on dangerous roads or in remote areas or in small airplanes, take a needle and suture kit and an HIV protection kit. The latter consists of an intravenous giving set and at least two liters of intravenous fluid. Be sure to get instructions as to how to use it.

- If you are allergic to bee stings or other insect stings, take an epinephrine auto-injector kit.

Check your health insurance coverage

If you are working for a large humanitarian agency, your health insurance will probably be arranged by the agency, but make sure. Whether the coverage is provided by the agency or some other source, make sure you are covered for medical expenses incurred outside of the country where the policy was issued. If you will be working in or traveling to a war zone, make sure that the insurance coverage remains in effect. Make sure your insurance covers medical evacuation to another country if necessary to obtain adequate care. (For possible sources of insurance, see Resources).

Blood transfusions are potentially dangerous

Contaminated blood is a major mode of transmission of HIV, Hepatitis B and Hepatitis C. If you will be stationed in or traveling for anything other than a short visit to an area where there is a high rate of HIV/AIDS, Hepatitis B or Hepatitis C, or if you will be traveling extensively on dangerous roads or in remote areas or in small airplanes, it is possible that a situation could arise in which you would need a blood transfusion. You may want to supplement your regular insurance with membership in The Blood Care Foundation in England (http://www.bloodcare. org.uk), which claims to get safe blood to members in almost any location in the world within 24 hours. You have to be a member to be eligible for this service. Both long term and short term memberships are available.

Be sure the clothing you are taking is appropriate

Be sure the clothing you are taking is appropriate for the climate and other health-related conditions. If you will be going to a hot area, take loose fitting cotton clothing, a hat for the sun, and closed shoes or boots (jigger fleas, hookworms and other parasites can enter through bare feet or open sandals). If you will be going to a cold area, take several layers of clothes (for example, shirt, sweater, jacket liner, warm jacket) rather than a single bulky layer. That way you can remove items if you start to get hot. And take a waterproof layer – raincoat, poncho or waterproof anorak – to wear over your clothes, along with a hat and boots.

Make basic travel arrangements

Obtain all necessary travel documents

- Passport –should have at least one to two years before expiration.

- National identity card – if applicable.

- Required visas and/or work permits.

- Organizational identification card.

- Driver's license.

- Medical insurance card.

- Letters of introduction.

- Yellow fever immunization certificate.

- Extra passport-size photos – at least six.

- Tickets.

- Make photocopies of all documents. Leave one copy at home with a family member or friend. Take another with you and keep it in a safe place separate from the originals. If you will be traveling with your family, it is a good idea to make photocopies of all of your passports on the same page. That way, if your passport is lost, there is evidence that you belong to the same family, which may facilitate travel or replacement of the lost passport.

Find out what you will need by way of money and make the appropriate arrangements. You may need cash (hard and/or local currency, as appropriate), a credit card, debit card or bank card for cash withdrawals at automatic teller machines, travelers' checks – find out what is the best currency, denomination, and offering bank, or personal checks. Note that travelers' checks are not acceptable everywhere and that automatic teller machines are not available in many countries. Make a list of all credit card numbers and the phone numbers for canceling them, should they be lost or stolen.

Be sure legal documents are up to date.

- Up-to-date will – make one if you do not already have one.

- Power of Attorney, left with someone you trust.

- Insurance policies – life, health, accident, disability: If you will be in or traveling through a conflict zone, check to be sure they will remain valid.

Leave a copy of your travel itinerary and contact information while away with family or friend, and make arrangements for ongoing communication by e-mail, telephone, mail, etc.

Do not forget the essentials:

- Pay outstanding bills and make arrangements to have continuing bills – for example, insurance premiums, mortgage payments, credit card bills and any loans – paid.

- Arrange for mail to be held or forwarded.

- Discontinue newspaper delivery, arrange for pets, etc.

Remember that travel plans for getting to your assignment do not consist only of planning for travel to the airport nearest your assignment. Find out where you are supposed to go once you get there and how you will get there. For example, how will you get from the airport to your hotel or work place? Make sure arrangements have been made for someone to meet you at the airport – especially if you will be arriving at night. Your travel plans should also include back-up plans in case the original plan does not work out. For example, you should know the name of a meeting place and how best to get there in case your agency/greeter misses you at the airport as you arrive.

What to take with you

In addition to your travel documents and money, credit cards, etc., take with you:

- A small bag or backpack – for day trips and other short excursions.

- Four or five changes of clothes. Be sure they are appropriate for the climate, the work you will be doing and the culture you will be living in. Be sure nothing looks remotely military.

- If you will be going to somewhere cold, take a sleeping bag.

- One set of 'dress-up', smart clothes.

- Closed shoes or boots.

- Outer garments – waterproof jacket; other seasonally appropriate clothing. Once again, be sure nothing looks remotely military.

- Towel and facecloth.

- Electrical equipment – portable cassette player or CD player, laptop computer, shaver, hair dryer, etc. Check that they will work with the voltage available in your destination country. If not, take appropriate converters and plug adaptors. In any case, take plenty of extra batteries – local power supplies may be unreliable.

- Stationery: paper, notebooks, pens and pencils, pencil sharpener, letter paper, envelopes.

- Medications, prescriptions, first aid kit, mosquito net and other medical and health-related supplies (see above, p. 19).

- Toiletries that may be hard to find: take shampoo, soap, toilet paper, facial tissues, brush and comb, razor and shaving soap, toothbrush, toothpaste, floss, nail clipper, liquid clothes detergent, tampons, contraceptives, contact lens cleaning supplies, lip balm, vitamins, etc.

- One change of clothes and basic toiletries to carry on the plane, in case your baggage gets mislaid.

- Unbreakable water bottle or canteen.

- References: technical reference books you may need for your work; maps; language guide or dictionary for local language; this guidebook.

- Other: calculator; supplies for leisure activities, such as books, cards, board games, binoculars, camera and film; hobby supplies such as paints, etc. Do not forget extra batteries, especially relatively uncommon sizes such as those used in cameras.

If you will be away only on a short mission (for example, consulting, training), travel as light as possible. Heavy luggage is a disaster.

CHAPTER 2

Safety and security in the field

The dangers of humanitarian work

Two basic principles for keeping safe
    Principle 1: up-to-date knowledge of the specific risks is essential
    Principle 2: prevention is better than response

Rules for traveling
    Before your trip
    During your trip
    When you arrive

Safety in motor vehicles
    Keep vehicles mechanically sound and appropriately equipped
    Follow motor vehicle laws and regulations
    While you are driving
    Driving in conflict zones and areas with land mines
    If you are involved in an accident

Safety on foot and on public transportation

Safety at home
    Privacy control: locks, doors and windows
    Building employees
    Fire safety
    Miscellaneous

Dealing with personal attacks or threats of attack
    If you are threatened with armed robbery or vehicle hijacking
    If you are threatened with kidnapping or are taken hostage

Weapons, land mines and military attacks
    Weapons
    Land mines
    If you come under military attack

Sexual assault and sexual harassment
    Avoiding or responding to sexual assaults
    Sexual harrassment

Note: The advice in this chapter is general in nature and can not cover every situation. The advice is intended to provide guidelines, not a straitjacket. There may be cases in which these recommendations do not provide the best course of action. You should seek out specific advice about the risks in the location of your assignment and you should seek out specific advice and/or training on how to deal with these risks.

Most humanitarian agencies have policies and procedures in place with respect to travel, driving, evacuation and other safety and security issues, and local field offices may have adapted these policies and procedures to local conditions. As an employee of an agency, you should, of course, learn and follow your employer's rules. The suggestions in this chapter should be used to supplement these rules, not replace them.

The material in this chapter has been digested from several more detailed manuals on safety and security prepared by various humanitarian organizations: *Safety First* (Save the Children); *Engineering in Emergencies* (RedR–Engineers for Disaster Relief); *Staying Alive* (International Committee of the Red Cross); *World Vision Security Manual* (World Vision International); *Security in the Field* (United Nations); and *Operational Security Management in Violent Environments* (Humanitarian Practice Network). Details of how to obtain these manuals can be found in Resources.

From an early age, we all learn rules to increase our safety and security in our usual environment – where the risks are, what the signs of danger are and how to respond to danger. 'Look both ways before you cross the street,' we tell our children. 'Don't take candy from strangers.' 'Don't play with matches.' 'Don't dive into water until you know how deep it is.' Working in a new environment, you may not know exactly what the rules are, what the places or activities to avoid are, what the signs of danger are or how to respond to various threats to your well-being. This chapter will help you 'relearn' rules of safety appropriate to your new environment.

The first part of the chapter discusses, in general terms, the risks of work on humanitarian projects of all kinds and some general principles for keeping safe. The remainder of the chapter consists of recommendations addressing specific kinds of risk: risks while traveling, driving, walking, or using public transportation; safety issues at home; personal attacks; military risks – including land mines; and risks that especially affect women.

You may object that some of the suggestions below seem unnecessarily cautious or that it is 'impractical' to carry out some of them. Before dismissing the recommendations too rapidly, remember that the environment in which humanitarian workers work has become an increasingly dangerous one. Over the last decade, at least 40 to 50 humanitarian workers have been killed in the line of duty every year, and many others have been injured. Other have been killed or injured in accidents or attacks not directly related to their work. Making matters worse, in recent years an increasing proportion of deaths among humanitarian workers are due to targeted attacks. About a third of these deaths occur in the first three months of service, and one in six occurred in the first 30 days of service. The higher level of risk early in an assignment is true for experienced field workers as well as for newcomers, since even the experienced worker may not be prepared for the specific dangers present in a new environment.

While it may be impractical to carry out all of the suggestions below, the more of them you can carry out, the more you reduce your risk. As you grow accustomed to your new environment, you will have a more accurate sense of which 'rules' can be broken and which should be followed religiously. Whatever the rules, there is no substitute for common sense and good judgment, based on knowledge of the local situation.

The dangers of humanitarian work

Forewarned is forearmed. The first step in protecting yourself is to understand the potential sources of danger.

Staff of humanitarian aid, development, and human rights projects face several sources of danger. First, there are the 'normal' risks and dangers of the local environment. *Just as at home, the biggest dangers are usually motor vehicles and street crime.* But on many assignments, these dangers are increased by several factors. Typically, humanitarian projects are carried out in poorer areas of the world. Resources to maintain roads and traffic control systems may be lacking. Many cars may be poorly maintained, with unsafe tires and worn out brakes, and many drivers may be inexperienced. Systems for maintaining law and order may, at best, be less efficient than you are used to; at worst, corrupt police and judicial systems and drunken soldiers may present a threat rather than a source of security. The contrast between desperate poverty and the *relative* affluence of humanitarian workers may make you a tempting target. For expatriates, cultural misunderstandings may lead to ordinary interpersonal interactions becoming more contentious than you expect.

Over and above these normal risks, the situations that create the need for humanitarian work – wars and civil wars, ethnic cleansing, refugee crises, natural disasters, famines, epidemics – create an additional set of risks. In the modern era, conflicts involving warlords, criminal gangs, terrorists and gun-carrying children replace the battles between traditional armies representing states that were characteristic of the past. Governmental control over the sources of organized violence may be weak and traditional social control mechanisms may break down. The physical and social infrastructure, ranging from hospitals and schools to police forces and courts, may be damaged or non-existent. Informal roadblocks or banditry may appear, along with threats from armed soldiers – some of them teenagers and/or drunk. Land mines or ongoing military action may be an ever-present danger. The emotional responses of local people, stressed out by a long series of traumatic events, often following in the wake of a long history of oppression – sometimes inflicted by the same country that is now sending humanitarian assistance – complicate all social interactions.

In the past, even in circumstances like these, the supposed neutrality and benevolence of humanitarian agencies provided their workers with some protection against danger. In recent years, NGOs and other agencies that provide humanitarian have increasingly themselves become direct targets of violence. Warlords may seek control of the resources provided by the aid organization or may extort support from aid organizations in return for 'protection' or as a condition of tolerating the organizations' activities. Bandits may kidnap humanitarian workers to obtain a ransom, or warlords may take hostages as a potential form of leverage against the government or against foreign powers. National governments, threatened by civil unrest, may forcibly seek to prevent aid from falling into the hands of its enemies. At a local level, aid organizations based in Europe and North America may seem a threat to traditional culture and mores and may be targeted by traditionalists.

Local (national) staff of humanitarian agencies may face some additional risks. One major risk is the increased exposure just from carrying out job duties: doing dangerous things, going places you might otherwise not visit, or engaging with people you might otherwise choose to avoid. In situations in which armed forces exist that are opposed to the work or even the presence of the agency, being known to be connected with the agency may be another source of risk. The access of a staff member to agency vehicles or communication equipment or other supplies may make you a tempting target, as does receiving a regular and presumably better-than-average salary. Local staff may also benefit less from the safety and security policies of their employer. All too often, training for local staff in safety and security measures is poor, inadequate or erratic; less attention is paid to providing physical protection for local staff – especially during off-duty hours; little attention is given to the safety of local staff-members' families; and local staff are left out of planning for emergency evacuation, should it be needed.

Because of the variety of situations in which humanitarian workers function, there are no universal rules. Each theatre of operations for an aid agency must be evaluated with regard to the overall level of risk. Each individual project and each job within the project must be evaluated with regard to the specific dangers that are presented. And each individual aid worker should make their own assessment of their own situation. What are the possible risks? Who might harm you? What are your vulnerabilities?

Two basic principles for keeping safe

There are two basic principles in protecting yourself: (1) up-to-date knowledge of the specific risks in a particular situation is essential; and (2) prevention is better than response.

Principle 1: Up-to-date knowledge of the specific risks is essential

In the past it was believed that working for a humanitarian organization was usually of itself a form of protection. Unfortunately, in many places, this principle and the advice following from it has been overtaken by world events:

Humanitarian organizations and their staff are increasingly direct targets for attack. Unfortunately, the advice stemming from the two different possibilities is diametrically opposed. If identification with a humanitarian organization provides legitimacy and protection, the best strategy would be to make your organizational identity very evident. Thus, many older books on safety and security have recommended marking the agency's vehicles very clearly with organizational insignia and names. But if identification with the organization endangers you, then your best strategy is to be as inconspicuous as possible. Thus, many organizations now try to use inconspicuous, local-made cars. It is crucial to make a hard-headed assessment of this issue. In general, in conflict and post-conflict situations, assume that you are potentially a target for attack. In more stable situations and non-conflict situations – for example, after a natural disaster – the old advice may still apply. Seek local advice.

It is also essential to find out what the particular risks are in a given environment apart from attacks targeted at you as a representative of a humanitarian organization. For example, in some countries, if an auto hits a pedestrian, the local people size up the situation and may decide to assault the driver. Knowing in advance that this kind of danger exists will determine your behavior in a crisis.

You may learn a lot about the local security situation from a distance, but the best sources of up-to-date information about potential or actual risks are local. Do not be afraid to ask. Your supervisor, co-workers, local staff of your agency, staff of other NGOs, local officials and local residents, even the armed forces, may be helpful sources of information about potential risks. International peacekeeping forces are also a good source. At the same time, always be skeptical of local security assessments. Often people who have worked or lived in a dangerous situation become numbed and do not assess very accurately how dangerous a context actually is. Listen, but do not be a slave, to local advice.

Also be aware that, however much you think you know about the dangers in your area, the situation can change rapidly. Risk assessment is an ongoing process. Be alert for shifts in the political or military situation. Be aware of changes in the behavior, attitudes or movements of the local population. Yesterday's risk may no longer be pressing; yesterday's zone of safety may be today's zone of danger. Being identified as a humanitarian worker, a source of safety yesterday, may be a source of danger today. Yesterday's 'reliable contact' may be today's betrayer.

Principle 2: Prevention is better than response

Your organization should have clear, unambiguous, easily accessible, practical, up-to-date *safety and security* policies and guidelines in place *before* an incident occurs. These should include, as appropriate, guidelines for the use of motor vehicles, access to buildings, interactions with the media, interactions with authorities and contingency plans for medical crises, armed attacks or a need to evacuate. Ask to see the policies, go over them carefully and *adhere to them rigorously*.

You should be briefed about the local situation and relevant safety and security precautions and procedures before starting your assignment. This briefing should be updated regularly. If you do not get it, ask for it. If you cannot get it, ask yourself whether this is a project you should be part of.

Briefing and training national staff on safety and security procedures is just as essential as briefing and training international staff. Most obviously, both national and expatriate staff face the same dangers and are deserving of the same protection. In addition, failure to brief each group endangers the other. For instance, the local driver who does not observe security procedures when driving endangers his passengers as well as himself. Expatriates who obliviously insist on going somewhere they should not go, ignoring the danger, endanger the local staff accompanying them. Local staff members are especially vulnerable to pressures from local authorities, political hard liners, criminal groups, disgruntled beneficiaries and others in the local community who do not have the interests of the agency or its staff at heart.

Think ahead. Be aware of the signs of danger in your location. Think through how you – individually or as a team – would respond to various unexpected contingencies. Rehearse your responses in potential danger situations. Anticipate where you could take shelter or get help if you needed to – for example, stores that are open late, police stations or public telephones.

Be prepared for the possibility of evacuation. Your agency should have a plan for how to evaluate and respond to dangers such as mounting terrorist activities, insurrections and other civil disorders, or natural disasters, and you should be familiar with that plan. But do not depend entirely on your agency. You should have your own personal evacuation plan for yourself and your family. It should include plans for scenarios in which the agency plan works and for scenarios in which it does not.

Consider the following questions in deciding what to do. Are you exposed to unreasonable risk? How imminent is the danger? Has it become impossible to meet project objectives due to security issues? How long is the danger likely to persist? Have the local or regional authorities recommended evacuation? Have the embassies advised their nationals to leave? What are the other NGOs and international organizations doing?

Remember that the opportunity to implement an evacuation plan may be brief and you may have to make your decisions and act quickly. Remember also that you have to be the ultimate judge of when to evacuate. Your own assessment of the danger and your own toleration for risk may differ from those of your agency director. Your own plan, like the agency plan, should include planning for possible evacuation routes – including border crossings; means of transportation to be used; personal documentation and currency needed; and what personal belongings and work-related materials you would take with you.

One major issue in deciding to leave may be the impact on national staff. Most agencies differentiate between the evacuation of expatriate and national staff. Most commonly, the agency does not evacuate national staff, though exceptions may be made and lesser measures, such as relocating national staff within the country of operation, may be taken. Expatriate staff may, understandably, be reluctant to leave local colleagues behind and expose them to dangers they are not willing to face. You may be forced to leave without prior goodbyes. This is a highly emotional issue for both national and international staff and, on the rare occasions when evacuations do take place, if it is mishandled it can dramatically increase risks to all staff and leave lingering resentment in their wake. Your agency should give thought ahead of time as to its ethical and practical responsibilities to national staff, but you, too, need to give thought ahead of time as to how much personal risk you are willing to take and how much risk you are prepared to accept for national staff and other local friends.

- Good communication with your colleagues is essential. Share experiences, concerns and information; combat rumors; and share ideas on how to improve safety. Chronic stress can lead people to make bad decisions or to exercise imprudent behaviors. Be aware of behaviors of other members of your team that can put them or others at risk, and do not be bashful about taking action to stop them. (See Chapter 5 for more about the signs of chronic stress.

- Build relationships with local staff and make other local friends. Local staff and friends are the first place to go for safety-related information. Local 'gossip' is often much more reliable than UN or international information. Beyond their usefulness as a source of information, local relationships are central to safety. Local residents who have their ears to the ground can give you early warnings of danger. It is relationships with local people that can protect you from attacks from others within the local community and sometimes from outside, as well.

- Err on the side of caution. If in doubt about the safety of an activity or trip, postpone it and seek more information. Follow your instincts – better embarrassed or inconvenienced than harmed.

- Be alert and aware of your surroundings at all times.

- Avoid behaviors that are likely to arouse suspicion or hostility or that expose you as a vulnerable target. Do not take photos or tape conversations without permission. Dress down. Be discrete about your possessions. Do not wear jewelry or an expensive watch. Avoid clothing styles that may offend local sensibilities. Avoid disputes or commotions in the street. Avoid situations that may arouse passions or elicit violence, such as political rallies. Do not present yourself publicly, for example, in discussions in a marketplace, as a national of a specific country when it is unnecessary to do so. Learn about practices that may be offensive in the local culture and monitor your behavior accordingly. Be especially careful about interactions with local people of the opposite sex.

- Think through the potential implications of any action that could be seen as 'taking sides' in local conflicts, such as attending political rallies.

- Learn skills that contribute to your own safety: first aid, use of radios and other communication equipment, vehicle operation and maintenance, land-mine awareness. Learn the local language – at the very least, enough to identify yourself as a worker for a humanitarian organization and to communicate a request for help.

■ If you think you are in immediate danger, it may make sense to call attention to yourself. Evaluate this advice in the specific context. In some situations, attracting attention may *increase* the danger. Shout, whistle, blow your horn, call for help. If you have to call for help, it is more effective to make a specific request, for example, 'Call the police right now!', than a general one, for example, 'Help, somebody help!' and, if possible, address your plea to a specific person or persons.

■ When you are in a foreign country, you are subject to its laws, not the laws of your home country. You can be arrested for actions that may either be legal or be minor infractions at home. Learn what is considered criminal in the country where you are. For example, there may be prohibitions on taking pictures of government buildings, border areas and transportation facilities. Drug transactions place you at especially great risk. Many countries do not distinguish between possession of drugs and trafficking. Possession of even small amounts of 'minor' drugs may be punished severely. Even some prescription drugs – particularly tranquilizers and amphetamines – are illegal in some countries. Be sure you understand the laws in the country of your assignment.

■ Remember: alcohol and drugs impair judgment.

■ Whatever the 'rules', do not be afraid to use common sense, good judgment and your knowledge of the local situation. The recommendations in this manual are guidelines, meant to help you protect yourself, not rigid rules to be followed no matter what the consequences.

Rules for traveling

Whenever you are traveling, whether to get to your assignment in the first place or on local trips while on your assignment, you are potentially vulnerable. The following principles will help reduce the risks.

Before your trip

Weigh the risks and the benefits of your trip. Define the aims of your trip. Is the trip really necessary? Find out as much as you can about the risks. Is the trip worth the risks?

Get security clearance for the trip planned from your agency and, if necessary, from local government or military officials.

Plan your travel itself:

■ Calculate the time needed to make your trip. Can the trip be done in the time you have? How will you get to your destination? If you will use public transportation, check schedules and connecting links.

- If it is a long trip, are there safe stopping places along the way? Many armed attacks occur at dusk or at night, so it is a good idea to plan to get off the road before dusk.

- How will you remain in communication during your trip? If by radio, be sure the radio is working and you know how to use it. If by cell phone, be sure there is service at appropriate points along your journey. If by pay phone, be sure you have change or an up-to-date phone card and that you know how to use the local phones. Carry emergency names, addresses and phone numbers.

- Have a plan what to do if you get stranded.

Think through who needs to accompany you on the trip and who should be informed about the trip. On long or difficult trips, do not travel alone. Be sure people at your destination know you are coming. Inform colleagues or the head of your mission or, when appropriate, local authorities of your plans.

Make sure that at least one other person – at home or at your starting point – knows where you are, where you are going, who you will be meeting with, where you will be staying and when you expect to return. If you are traveling from one location to another, make sure someone at your destination knows when you will arrive and is instructed to let the designated person at home or in your home office know if you do not arrive when scheduled. Be sure to let both your home office and the person at your destination know if your plans change.

Do not discuss your travel plans with strangers. Do not go off with strangers. Beware of unmarked cabs – only take licensed taxis. If you do take a taxi, try to ensure that a colleague at your departure point sees you off and could recognize the driver.

During your trip

Remain in communication, while en route and when you arrive. If your travel plans change while you are en route, be sure to let whoever is monitoring your travel at home and the person expecting you at your destination know of the changes. If you will be gone for more than a day, work out a plan for you to call a designated person (supervisor, spouse or partner, friend, etc.) every 24 hours. Your failure to call by the appointed time should trigger calls to emergency contacts.

Carry appropriate documents, including your organizational identification papers, drivers license, a copy of your passport and, if appropriate, a letter from your organization – in English and in the local language – that describes the organization and its purpose and describes the purpose of your trip. Note that in some areas, a *copy* of your passport may not be acceptable – you may be required to carry the original of all identification documents. Check on local rules.

Be especially careful about traveling at night. Avoid night travel altogether if at all possible. Get off the road before dusk. If you must travel at night, keep to well-lit, well-traveled roads and well populated streets.

Do not accept food or beverages from strangers or accept rides from strangers. Watch your luggage. Hard case luggage may be less liable to tampering, but if you will have to carry it for any distance, you will be happier with lighter weight bags. All luggage should be labeled with your name and address inside and outside. Use covered tags for outside labels, so that a casual observer cannot see your name and address.

Carry the minimal amount of money or other valuables needed for your trip. Leave your cash and credit cards in a secure place at home. If you do need to carry valuables, do not carry them all in one wallet or purse. Instead, divide them up, in different pockets or bags. Do not place valuables in handbags, fanny packs (waist-worn pouches) or easily accessible outside pockets, Use inside pockets, pouches or money belts worn under your clothing, or a sturdy shoulder bag worn across your chest, not just over your shoulder.

To avoid problems at customs, keep medicines in original, labeled containers. Bring copies of your prescriptions and, in case there is any question, a letter from your physician explaining your need for the medication.

You are vulnerable to pickpockets and theft in public areas such as waiting rooms and airline terminals, tourist sites, market places and festivals. Be especially cautious and try to minimize your time in such areas. Try to schedule direct flights or trains rather than routes that require transfers. Beware of strangers who approach you offering bargains or asking for directions or for the time, who jostle you, who point to something spilled on your clothing, or who distract you by creating a disturbance. Even a child or a woman carrying a baby can be a pickpocket. Beware of groups of children who create a distraction while picking your pocket.

Be selective about which hotel or restaurants you use. For example, a restaurant that serves lots of alcohol in a fervent Muslim context is a convenient target for attack, as is a restaurant frequented mainly by expatriates.

When you arrive

Know ahead of time how you will get from the airport or other transportation terminal to your hotel or first appointment. If you are being met, be sure the person meeting you has proper identification. Check beforehand if the local taxis are reliable. Discuss fares before getting into the taxi. Do not use an unlicensed taxi or accept a ride with a stranger.

Be aware of people possibly posing as security or police. Do not accompany them to another place without obtaining and verifying their identification. If you will be staying in a hotel, try to use larger hotels, which provide greater security.

- Avoid ground floor and top floor rooms, which are easier for strangers to gain access to. If possible, choose a room near the elevator.

- Be alert to the possibility of being followed to your room. If you are alone, do not get in to an elevator if there is a suspicious looking person inside. If you find the door to your room unlocked, do not enter. Go to the main desk and ask someone to accompany you to the room. When you enter the room, check the closets, bathroom and balcony to be sure no one is there.

■ When you first get into your room, check to see if the room phone works. Note the evacuation routes to use in case of fire or other emergency and the locations of fire escapes or fire stairs.

■ Keep your door locked, even when you are in the room, and keep the curtains closed, especially at night. Do not open your door to callers unless you have identified them by phone or by the peephole in the door. Meet visitors you do not know well in the lobby.

■ Do not leave valuables in your room. Use the hotel safe deposit box instead.

Inform your home contact person that you have arrived. If there are any changes in where you will be staying or in your return plans, be sure to let them know.

Safety in motor vehicles

Motor vehicle accidents are the most common causes of death and injury to staff of humanitarian projects. Whether you are the driver or a passenger, wear your seatbelt at all times. Most car accident injuries can be prevented or made less serious by wearing a seatbelt. This is the single most important effective measure to keep you safe in a car.

Motor vehicle incidents can occur when you are driving as part of your job or when you are driving for personal reasons. Note that it will often be the case that you will not yourself be the driver of the vehicle you are traveling in. Very frequently, agencies hire local residents as drivers, for a variety of reasons. If so, do not simply assume that the driver of your vehicle is familiar with and observes these rules: check.

If you will be using a driver, check on local etiquette. Who pays the driver? How do you make requests and determine routes? Do you maintain a formal relationship or become friendly if you have the same drivers over and over? What do you do about waiting? How do you work with the driver if you have to pass through security checkpoints? Can you expect the driver to also act as an interpreter and guide on local safety issues or to provide suggestions about where to eat, stay, etc.?

Keep vehicles mechanically sound and appropriately equipped

■ Have a regular maintenance schedule for any vehicles you drive and follow it. Check the oil, coolant, fuel supply, tire pressure regularly. Have the oil changed and the car tuned up at appropriate intervals.

■ Always keep the fuel tank at least half full.

■ Keep emergency supplies in the car. This should include supplies for you – for example, first aid kit, food, water, flashlight, maps, blanket – and supplies for the car – for example, a spare tire, in good shape and properly inflated; a jack and tools for changing a tire; all necessary documentation; a tool kit and an extra fan belt. Be sure you have the right jack and tools for your car and that you know how to use them.

■ Be sure your vehicle is well marked with the logo of your organization or an organizational flag, *except in places where the organization may be a specific target of attack*. Avoid using vehicles that look like the kinds of military vehicles used in your area.

Follow motor vehicle laws and regulations

■ Be sure auto documents and your driver's license are valid and up to date. Be sure vehicle documents are in the car and that you are carrying your driver's license.

■ Respect local traffic regulations and laws. Drive especially slowly through villages and other populated areas.

■ Be patient and courteous toward traffic authorities and local officials, even when you think they are wrong.

While you are driving

■ Know your vehicle. Take your time getting used to a vehicle you have not driven before. If the vehicle has four-wheel drive, learn how to engage it.

■ Before entering, or re-entering, your car, check underneath the car from a distance and look inside for possible intruders. Be aware of any suspicious activity around the car

■ Beware. Roads may be in bad condition and road signs may be missing. You may encounter inexperienced drivers or drivers with a different sense of the rules of the road and of driving etiquette than you are used to. Or you may find traffic sparse, which means there will not be anyone around to help if you have difficulties.

■ Many people who are safe drivers 'at home' throw caution to the winds when away. Although it should not need to be said, no driving at high speed, no passing recklessly, and always wear your seatbelt.

■ In urban areas or other populated areas where you may be driving slowly or stopping, keep your doors locked at all times. Keep windows open only an inch or two at the top for ventilation. Be especially alert at red lights and stop signs. Try to adjust your speed to avoid having to stop at intersections.

■ Flying objects can be dangerous. If you are driving in an area where there may be land mines, drive with the windows open – imploding glass can be deadly. Strap all loose objects – boxes, first aid kits – to the sides and floor of the car.

■ Do not pick up hitchhikers or offer rides to strangers.

- Try to choose routes that will avoid checkpoints and roadblocks. If you do come to a roadblock:
  - Slow down. Turn off your radio and open the window part way so that you can hear instructions. (Caution: In some locales you are expected to open your window, but in others, opening the window all the way may be seen by those manning the roadblock as a sign of hostility. Find out what the local 'rules' are). Dip your headlights as you approach; switch to sidelights (parking lights) and turn on the inside (dome) light when you stop. Leave your motor running unless you are told to shut it off. Keep valuables, including cigarettes, gum, and candy, out of sight.
  - Always obey an order or signs to stop. Do not drive on until you are instructed to do so. Do not make radio transmissions. Keep your hands visible and do not make sudden moves. Do not reach for the glove box without letting those manning the checkpoint know what you are doing. Stay in the car if you can. If ordered to leave it, stay close to car.
  - Act confident but not cocky or belligerent. Answer all questions as accurately and courteously as possible, but do not talk too much or too rapidly. Do not be in a rush. Be prepared to chat. Do not offer cigarettes or gum or candy. Do not argue with those manning the checkpoint. If you feel their behavior is inappropriate, ask a senior official of your agency to take the matter up with the appropriate local or military authority.
  - Show your identification papers if requested to do so and explain where you are going. You may want to briefly summarize your organization's work. Do not surrender your ID, unless forced to do so.
  - Be relaxed if those manning the checkpoint insist on checking your vehicle. If they demand to search the vehicle, protest but do not resist. Stay close and watch any search, to be sure nothing is planted in the vehicle. If any items are removed, protest but do not resist.
  - Resist pressure from those manning a checkpoint to give a lift to a stranger. Be especially insistent about not allowing people carrying arms into your car. Explain that it is organizational policy. In areas where there is ongoing conflict and/or presence of armed groups, you may want to consider having a decal on the door or window saying that guns are not permitted in the vehicle.

- If you come to a new, improvised, unofficial or unauthorized roadblock, be very wary. Stop well before the roadblock to assess the situation. Watch what happens to other cars going the same direction as you. Ask drivers of vehicles coming your way who have already passed through the roadblock what is going on. If you have any doubts, turn around and drive away.

- If someone tries to force you off the road, do not panic. Blow your horn continuously to try to call attention to yourself. If forced over, stop, back up, and keep driving.

- If you think you are being followed, do not drive home. Drive around on an active street. If you still think you are being followed, drive to a secure place for help, such as a police station.

- Carjackers and thieves may operate at gas stations, parking lots, in city traffic or along the highway. Be suspicious of anyone who flags you down or hails you or tries to get your attention when you are in your car or near it.

- Before getting out of your car, look around. Check for loiterers or other possible sources of danger. If in doubt, do not get out. Always lock your car when you leave it. If you will be returning to your car after dark, park it in a place that will be well lit when you return.

Driving in conflict zones and areas with land mines

If you *must* drive in an area that is especially dangerous, travel in a convoy, if possible. A leader should be assigned for each vehicle and for the convoy as a whole. Keep vehicles two to three car lengths apart. Maintain radio communication between vehicles – especially between the lead and trailing car – and between the convoy and your field office. Keep in regular touch with the relevant local authorities, before your trip, to ensure that you are up to date on the military situation. If appropriate, notify local authorities or military authorities along your route of your movements to avoid surprising them.

If you are driving in an area where there is a risk of land mines, see pp. 42–45.

If you are involved in an accident

- Quickly assess the attitudes and actions of people around the scene of the accident.

- Provide first aid and transportation to the hospital for anyone injured.

- Do not leave the scene of the accident unless you believe that to remain would place you in danger. If you must leave, drive directly to the nearest police station or military post. If the situation is safe, someone from your party should remain to provide details of the accident and report to the police, if appropriate.

Safety on foot and on public transportation

- Seek advice about areas you should avoid. Do not assume that, because the area 'looks safe,' it is safe. Unless you are certain you will be in a safe area, do not walk alone.

- Know where you are going, or at least *look like* you know where you are going. Consult your map *before* you leave home or in a non-public place.

- Before going out, make sure your purse, briefcase or other bag is closed. Carry handbags with a strap by crossing the strap across your body, not just over one shoulder. Do not carry your wallet in your hip pocket. Carry it in a front pocket, preferably with a button or other closure, or carry it under your clothes.

- Divide your money up. Carry 'mugger money' in one pocket and split up the rest of your money in several pockets. Avoid carrying credit cards or other important documents you will not need on the particular trip. Do carry your ID.

- Always remain alert and aware of your surroundings. Do not 'space out.' Use a route that takes you through well lit locations. Do not take short cuts. Avoid deserted areas. Walk near the curb, away from bushes or dark doorways or other possible places of concealment. If you use a 'Walkman' or other personal sound system, keep the volume low so that you can hear noises in your environment.

- If a driver pulls up beside you – for example, 'to ask for directions' or to 'offer you a ride' – be cautious. Do not get too close to the vehicle. Beware of requests (for example, 'Look at this map') that would force you to do so. Do not hitchhike or accept rides from strangers.

- If someone suspicious is behind you, cross the street. Do it again if necessary. If think you are being followed, draw attention to yourself. It is better to be embarrassed than attacked.

- If you are using public transportation, wait for vehicles in the designated waiting areas, especially at night. Do not ride deserted buses or trains or trolleys. On trains, sit in a non-deserted car near the middle of the train. On trolleys or buses, sit near the motorman or conductor. After getting off the vehicle, be sure you are not followed.

- It is easy to get wrong information. Do not ask questions about travel that can be answered with a 'yes' or 'no', for example, 'Is this the bus to X'? 'Is this the way to Y'? You may get a 'yes' that simply means the person you are asking wanted to be agreeable or simply didn't understand you. Instead, ask an open-ended question, for example, 'Where is this bus going?' or 'How do I get to Y'?

Safety at home

We all want to feel that home is a place of safety, a place where we do not have to always be on the alert, a place where we can 'let our guard down.' To make that be a reality, not just a sign of wishful thinking, takes some forethought.

Privacy control: locks, doors, and windows

- Doors should be strong, have a good lock, and have a peephole and safety chain. Keep the door to your apartment or house locked, even when you are inside for just a few minutes.

- Manage keys properly. Keep the number to the minimum needed. Know and control who has a key. If your key gets lost under circumstances in which someone could identify whose key it is, have a new lock installed. Do not keep your name or address on your key chain. Do not leave keys for friends or for emergency use in obvious hiding places.

- Do not open the door to anyone you have not positively identified, either by an intercom, peephole or with the safety chain in place. Be wary about unexpected visitors. Do not permit a stranger to come in to use your phone, even in an 'emergency.' (You might offer to make a call for him or her, instead).

- Keep windows locked, unless you have bars installed to prevent entry. At night, you are easily visible from outside. Keep curtains drawn or blinds or shades pulled down.

- Make a nightly safety check before bed. Be sure all doors and windows are properly locked.

Building employees

- Screen all prospective servants and security guards. Be sure to get references and full identifying information about them. Be sure servants and security guards know your security rules, such as not opening the door to strangers without specific approval from you, even if the stranger says that you said it was all right to let them in; not providing any information about you or your family; alerting you of any suspicious event or if any stranger asks about you or requests admission.

Fire safety

- Be sure your home is equipped with fire extinguishers, that they are properly charged (check periodically), and that you know how to use them.

- Periodically check your home, including basement and attic, for flammable fluids, oily rags, unsafe electrical wiring or electrical appliances.

- Know where the fire exits are. Make sure doors to fire exits are kept unlocked, from the inside. Have a plan for how you would escape and practice it.

- Be sure smoke detectors are installed and properly maintained. Replace the batteries regularly. In a multiple unit dwelling – hotel, apartment house – be sure there are fire sirens or bells – both automatic and manually operated.

Miscellaneous

- Make it easy to see if anyone is lurking near your door. Install outdoor lighting around the entrance area. Cut back bushes close to the door.

- Install a telephone if your apartment does not have one, or get a cell phone, if service is available, or get a radio or other means of communicating with the world outside your apartment in an emergency.

- Do not enter an elevator if there is someone suspicious already in it or who appears to be getting in with you. Invent an excuse. When in the elevator, stand near the control panel. If you feel threatened, push the alarm and as many of the 'floor' buttons as you can, so that the doors will open at every floor.

■ Know where the fuse box or circuit breaker panel is. Keep emergency light and/or power sources on hand – candles, flashlights, emergency generators.

Dealing with personal attacks or threats of attack

If you are threatened with armed robbery or vehicle hijacking

■ Try not to exacerbate the situation. Armed assailants are most likely to use their weapon if they feel their own safety is threatened. Try to remain calm and avoid panic. Maintain a polite, confident demeanor. Do not be aggressive or argumentative or try to intimidate the assailant(s). Speak slowly, calmly and distinctly. Make sure your hands are visible. Move slowly, with precise gestures. Avoid direct eye contact with your assailant(s). Be cooperative. Put your hands up, if told to do so. If you are in a group, do not talk among yourselves more than is necessary. Be especially careful about talking in a language your assailant(s) may not understand.

■ Don't be a 'hero': It is not heroic to risk your life or physical well-being to protect property.

■ If you are in a car when you are stopped and assailed, engage the hand brake but keep the motor running. Try to stay in the car. If you are forced out, leave the door open. Allow the hijacker to depart without interference.

■ *Unless you have reason to believe you are being targeted specifically because you work for a humanitarian organization*, you may want to identify yourself and your organization to the assailant(s).

■ Do not try to escape unless you are sure you will succeed or unless you are virtually certain that you face imminent death or serious physical harm if you do not try.

■ Observe as much as you can about your attackers, to be able to identify them at a later time.

If you are threatened with kidnapping or are taken hostage

■ The first few minutes of a hostage taking situation are the most dangerous. Your captors will be in a state of high emotional arousal and may behave irrationally. Take a deep breath and try to relax. Accept the situation and obey instructions promptly. Do not volunteer information. Avoid staring at your captors.

■ Do not try to escape unless your life is in imminent danger. It is extremely risky. If you fail, it can lead to a serious worsening of the conditions under which you and others are held. Even if you succeed, it can seriously jeopardize others being held hostage.

■ When things settle down, identify yourself and your organization to your captors. Encourage them to communicate with your organization or with local authorities.

- Try to keep a low profile and try to maintain your sense of personal dignity. Do not make threats. Obey commands without seeming servile. Do not beg, plead or cry. Try to remain inconspicuous, but listen and observe. If you are in a group, appoint one person to be the spokesperson for everyone, so as to present a common front and not give your captors an opportunity to play you and your co-hostages off against each other.

- Prepare yourself mentally for what could be a long ordeal. Be patient. Consciously focus on keeping yourself calm and preventing yourself from becoming disoriented or confused. Think about a pleasant memory or visualize a pleasant scene, pray, meditate. (Some self-calming techniques are discussed in detail in Chapter 5). Exercise your memory: recall a favorite poem, do mathematics problems in your head, or recall the plot of a book you have read or a movie you have seen. If possible, try to maintain a routine. Keep track of time. Maintain standards of tidiness and cleanliness.

- Eat what you are given, even if it is not appealing. A loss of weight and appetite is normal. Keep physically active; even if you are confined, do stretching exercises and calisthenics. Try to get enough sleep. Keeping up your strength is important.

- Try to build a rapport with your captors. If they can see you as human, you are in less danger. Draw attention to your own and others' human needs – for food, water, use of toilet, sleeping accommodation. Do not be afraid to ask for anything you need or want, such as books, paper and pencils or medicines. Find areas of mutual interest with your captors, such as family or children or sports. Avoid politics or other confrontational subjects. Remember that you are being held because you are valuable to your captors. It is important for them to keep you alive and well.

- Be aware of the 'Stockholm Syndrome', named after a case in which several hostages imprisoned for six days by criminals in a Swedish bank vault found themselves seeing the criminals as their protectors and the police as the enemy. It is not uncommon for those held prisoner for several days to identify with their captors and even defend them. Also be aware that feelings of depression, helplessness, humiliation, and anxiety are common. Resist them but do not feel bad about having such feelings – they are normal, not a sign of weakness.

- If there is a rescue attempt, drop to the floor. Try to reach cover. Keep your hands over your head.

Weapons, land mines and military attacks

If you are working in a region where there is or recently has been military conflict, it is important to develop a basic understanding of military issues and terminology. Learn about the local command structure, who the most important person in a unit is, the kinds of munitions used locally and the locations of local military camps or bases.

Weapons

Under most circumstances, you are safer as a clearly unarmed person than you are with a weapon. Do not allow weapons or live ammunition inside your organization's building or vehicles – save in accord with the organization's policy or when carried by officially approved guards. Do not allow soldiers or other armed people to ride in your car. Consider having a sticker on the window or door stating that this is organizational policy.

Do not collect ammunition – for example, unexploded shells – as a form of memorabilia. It can go off unexpectedly, killing or injuring bystanders. Avoid getting in the direct line of fire of any weapon, loaded or not, even if it is carried by a guard or lying on the floor. If threatened with a firearm, take no chances, even if it means handing over property. Bullets go faster than you can run.

Land mines

Land mines and unexploded ordnance are a widespread and serious danger to anyone working in a conflict or post-conflict area, not only when a conflict is in progress but for many years after. Thirty years after the end of the war in Vietnam, children are still being killed by previously unexploded mines.

- Seek out training in land mine recognition and awareness. This should include learning to recognize the appearance of the types of mines common in your area, how to detect possibly mined areas, general precautions and emergency procedures if you have to get out of a mine field.

- Learn as much as possible about the local land mine situation, so that you can avoid high risk areas. Sources of information may include colleagues, land mine clearing teams, local military authorities, local civilian authorities, UN staff and staff of other NGOs, public transportation officials and workers, hospitals, those manning checkpoints and local residents.

- Learn to recognize the minefield markers used locally, including both 'official' markers placed by mine clearing teams or local authorities and the informal markers used by local residents.

- Be alert for clues that there may be mines. These may include battlefield relics; animal remains; deserted buildings or abandoned vehicles; 'odd' looking bushes or out-of-place trees; tangles of wire; wooden stakes – especially in conjunction with wire; objects of unusual colors or shapes; dirty yellow or green objects; or recent patches in the road. Inspect any suspicious objects from a distance. (Binoculars may come in handy). Do not proceed across a possibly mined area if you are not sure it is safe.

- *Never* touch a suspected mine or unexploded shell, or other suspicious or 'interesting' object on the ground or try to move it. Do not even go close – there may be a trip wire that you do not see.

- Before setting out on a journey in an area where there is a risk of mines, always check *that day* with whatever agency is responsible for local mine clearance.

- *Never* allow yourself to be the first vehicle of the day to use a stretch of road in a high risk area. Observe the road to see if it is used by local people or to see if other vehicles are using it without incident.

- Stay on well-traveled, well-worn roads and paths. Do not drive across fields or on dirt paths not usually traveled by motor vehicles. Avoid the edges of a road. Be alert for fresh 'road repairs'. Follow in human or animal or vehicle tracks. Do not drive at night, if possible. Do not try to pass or turn around on the shoulder of the road. Keep off the shoulder of the road, even to overtake or get by another vehicle.

- If you are in a car and you suspect the road ahead is mined – or if you have to turn around for any other reason – do *not* turn around by moving forward. Back up slowly. Do not get out of your vehicle. Wait until you reach a place where you do not have to go onto the shoulder to turn around.

- If you are walking, do not explore abandoned ruins or vehicles or gardens or orchards. Do not take off-road 'shortcuts'. If you are in a group, walk single file with 10 to 20 meters between each person.

- If you identify one mine, there are probably more in the same area. Treat the whole area as a minefield.

If, despite these precautions, you find yourself in a suspected minefield:

1 *Stop.* Stand still. Stay there as long as it takes for someone to come along to assist. You should have filed some kind of travel plan, so if you are overdue, a rescue plan should kick into operation. Waiting the whole night or even several days is preferable to spending the rest of your life on crutches. If you see what you think is a mine, *do not touch it.*

2 If, despite this warning, you elect to try to get out on your own, identify the nearest safe area – for example, a paved road or well-traveled path. Carefully check the ground around your feet. Look carefully for signs of disturbance in the ground, visible trip wires and the like around you and between you and the presumably safe area. Walk *one* step toward the safe area. Repeat this procedure until you reach safety. After leaving the minefield, mark it with a sign and report it to your agency and to local authorities.

3 If someone else is caught in a mine field, *get help.* Do not try to rescue them. Where there is one mine, there are probably more. Even if someone is injured and calling for help, the best thing to do is to leave them there until you have a professional mine clearance team available. It is not a good idea to try to work your way through the mines to get the person out. The risk that you will become a second victim is very high and moving an injured person is extremely difficult as well as dangerous. Of course, imagine that the injured person is your best friend or your spouse, calling for help. It would be hard not to go to help and you will have to make a difficult decision. But it is intensely dangerous, for you and for them.

If you come under military attack

If the armed attack is not specifically aimed at you or your organization
Try to remain calm and avoid panic. Try to make yourself, your staff, your car, your building identifiable to the attackers. If you are in a car, stop. Reverse to show that your intent is to leave. Then turn around and drive away slowly. If you go forward to turn around, you may be perceived as attacking. If you are not in a vehicle, you will have to decide whether to go or to stay put. Usually, unless you are in an exposed place, it is safer to stay put and wait until the fighting subsides. Try to take shelter behind a wall or inside a building. Keep clear of windows. Stay together. Try to find out what is happening. You may get clues from the attitudes and behavior of the local population.

If an ambush or other attack has you or your vehicle as the intended target
Use your car as a defensive weapon. If the attackers are beside you or behind you, accelerate. If attacked from ahead, stop, reverse, turn around and flee. If your vehicle is immobilized and under fire, get out and dive for cover. Do not look up and do not try to take cover under the vehicle.

If you are in an area that is being bombed or shelled
If you are on foot, take immediate cover: If you are in a vehicle, get out and take cover on the ground, not under the vehicle. Keep your keys and radio with you. Lie flat, face down. Protect your eardrums with your hands and keep your mouth slightly open to equalize the pressure. If possible, crawl to a more protected place – a ditch, a culvert, behind a wall, in a building. Leave only when the bombing or shelling stops.

If a grenade is thrown at you
Turn in the opposite direction, take one or two giant steps and dive to the ground. Lie face down, legs crossed, body straight, head away from grenade, arms beside your legs. The reason for keeping your arms down rather than using them to cover your head is that shrapnel through the sides of the body tends to cause more serious injuries than to the head, especially if you throw yourself down with your feet closest to the grenade and head furthest away. Do not try to keep running – you have only a few seconds and shrapnel moves faster than you can run.

Sexual assault and sexual harassment

All women, regardless of age or physical appearance, are potential victims of sexual harassment and assault. More often than is commonly appreciated, men, too, are sexually assaulted or harassed. Expatriates should remember that local cultural assumptions about appropriate behavior for women may differ markedly from those you are familiar with at home. A professional woman carrying out professional activities may in itself be a source of tension, and modes of dress, innocent gestures, interactions with men and other behaviors to which you give little thought may also be sources of misunderstanding. The response patterns you are used to at home can not be counted on.

Most of the suggestions discussed above on safety at home and while traveling will reduce the risk. Some additional, more specific precautions may also be helpful.

Avoiding or responding to sexual assaults

- Dress and act conservatively and avoid conspicuous displays of jewelry or cash: Many sexual assaults are 'opportunistic', carried out during the commission of another crime – for example, a robbery. Learn local customs and expectations about dress and behavior, especially dress and behavior with the opposite sex. Learn about areas to avoid.

- Follow your instincts. If you feel uncomfortable about a person or situation, leave. If you feel in danger, call attention to yourself: scream, sound your horn, blow a whistle. Learn enough of the local language to call for help. Know the words for 'police,' 'fire,' etc. A call of 'fire' may be an effective way of getting attention and assistance, even if, strictly speaking, it is inappropriate.

- Be cautious with people you do not know. But be aware that *most sexual assaults are committed not by strangers but by people known to the victim,* including casual acquaintances, neighbors, dates and family members.

- Know where local places of safety are – for example, police stations, stores that are open late, and movie theaters.

- For long term housing, consider living with roommates.

- If you are a single woman, consider wearing a 'wedding ring'. An unmarried woman acting in a way that is unconventional by local standards may be a target. However, should you choose this strategy, note that if you subsequently engage in a relationship – friendly or intimate – with another man once your married status has been 'established', you may be seen as promiscuous, which creates new dangers.

- Rehearse your possible responses to confrontations. There is no universal answer as to whether it is best to try to talk your way out of a threatened assault, shout, flee, fight or submit – if you feel that not to do so would risk serious or life-threatening injury. Another alternative may be 'passive resistance' – talking or acting in ways that make you a less desirable target or increase the perpetrator's fear of consequences.

Whether to report a sexual assault to the police is a personal decision and may present new and painful challenges. The response of local police may be respectful and professional and they may treat you with dignity, but in other instances they may be less sensitive. If the rapist is caught and you choose to prosecute, you may face a new ordeal. You will have to confront your assailant and he may try to raise embarrassing aspects of your own past as a defense.

If you do report a rape to the police, you will be asked to undergo a physical examination. You should do nothing to destroy evidence of the attack, including washing yourself or your clothing, until you have been examined.

Regardless of whether or not you choose to report a sexual assault to the police, you should be aware that sexual assaults have both short-term and long-term emotional effects. There is no one 'right' way to respond. The immediate effects may include feelings of shock and disbelief; fear, anger and anxiety; super-alertness to further possible danger; or a kind of superficial calm and sense of being 'disconnected' from oneself and from the events. Physical symptoms such as disruption of sleep, gastro-intestinal problems, muscular tension, headaches, fatigue, as well as the direct physical effects of the assault may persist for weeks. Even long after the attack, feelings of guilt, self-blame, anger or depression may remain. Many women report nightmares, fear of certain places, sexual fears, extreme depression, insomnia, difficulty concentrating or apathy. These responses are not a sign of 'going crazy.' They are completely normal, though they may be enormously distressing. They are much like the emotional effects of other kinds of traumatic events, which are discussed at greater length in Chapter 5. One part of protecting yourself from such long term effects is to talk about the assault as much as possible with friends and family or to someone else you trust.

Your agency has a clear moral obligation to provide you with the emotional, practical and legal support you need in such a crisis. It should know the local laws regarding rape and should be prepared to advise you on how rapes are handled by the local police, prosecutors and media. It should also provide you with professional counseling, if you desire it. A good source of additional detailed information on rape and responding to rape is the US Peace Corps *Rape Response Handbook*, available online at http://www.lmu.edu/globaled/peacecorps/rape.html.

Sexual harassment

Sexual harassment is the term used to describe stares, leers, jokes, comments, graffiti, whistles, crude remarks, muttered obscenities, unwanted minor physical contacts, inappropriate personal questions, unwelcome sexual advances, requests for sexual favors and other behaviors that people use to terrorize or intimidate others without physically assaulting them. On the street these actions may create fear, anger, a sense of vulnerability, feelings of humiliation or a sense of degradation. In the workplace, they may create an intimidating, hostile or offensive environment and interfere with work. Sometimes submission to these behaviors – or, in more extreme cases, compliance with sexual advances – may be made an explicit or implied condition for promotion or employment. While sexual harassment usually consists of behaviors by men aimed at women, sometimes the behaviors may be aimed at other men, as well.

Sexual harassment is contrary to the provisions of the United Nations Charter and is contrary to the policies of many NGOs. In some countries it is against the law, but in many countries it is tolerated or even culturally encouraged.

Your reactions to harassment may help to defuse or exacerbate the situation.

- The overriding rule for response is to stay out of danger.

- On the street, if you feel you are reasonably safe, several responses are possible, depending on the circumstances and your own preferences. You may wish to ignore the behavior or you may wish to assert yourself by making your displeasure and your wish for the behaviors to cease clear.

- If the harassment occurs at work or if the harasser is a co-worker, take time to think about what you would like the outcome of any action to be. Find out about your rights in your organization. Think about the risks involved in any course of action. What has worked for others is not necessarily what would work best for you. Do not ignore harassment at work. It will not go away by itself. There are several possible courses of action.
  - One alternative is to let your objections to the harassment be known. Make it clear to the harasser that you do not like what he is doing. If he persists, report the unwanted behavior to your supervisor (if he is not the perpetrator) or to higher levels of management (if your supervisor is the perpetrator). If a verbal complaint does not get results, follow it up with a written complaint.
  - Since the men harassing you may be people that you have to work with – as colleagues or as people in the community – and that you need to maintain the respect of, simply calling in the authorities may create new problems. If the harassment is relatively minor – for example, verbal harassment, without personal intrusiveness, physical contact or threat of retaliation if you don't respond – some women decide to treat it as banter and engage it directly. One veteran worker recalled a colleague who called out to her: 'Why don't you come over and I'll take care of you, since your husband is so far away?' She responded, 'What makes you think you could take care of me?' The banter escalated, but her stance was that she was too much for him and that he would not be worth her effort. At the end of the exchange, she reports, she had actually increased the respect she received from male colleagues. Similarly, minor physical contact can be responded to with a 'don't be naughty' look and a shake of the head, while smiling, followed by making sure not to sit or stand next to the offender in future settings. This stance has some risk, but if you feel safe and feel able to pull it off, it is a possible alternative.
  - Document your experience. Keep a log, noting who the harasser was, the date, the event and the names of witnesses. Keep documents that support your side of the story – for example, copies of good work evaluations, records of complaints and of correspondence.
  - Do not try to deal with sexual harassment alone. Share your experience with others you trust. This will help you feel less isolated, is potentially a source

of advice and may help corroborate your complaints at a later time if you make a formal complaint.

■ Do not brood about the events. Release your feelings of anger and indignity in a safe environment so you can put the immediate incident out of your mind as quickly as possible.

CHAPTER 3

Taking care of yourself: preventing health problems in the field

Preventing exposure to the environmental causes of illness
Avoiding contaminated water
Avoiding contaminated food
Avoiding insect-borne disease
Preventing person-to-person transmission of disease
Preventing exposure to miscellaneous other health problems

Keeping your defenses up: acting to keep your immune system strong
Nutrition and hydration
Sleep, rest and relaxation
Exercise
Maintaining malaria prophylaxis and other immunizations
Stress

Keeping things from getting worse
Medical care, injections, transfusions and medicines
Fevers
Diarrhea
Cuts and bruises

Note: The information and advice in this chapter are general in nature. You should seek out specific advice from a qualified medical professional about the particular risks you as an individual face in the specific location where your assignment will be. You should also seek professional medical advice if you have specific health concerns before leaving for your assignment or if you have specific health concerns while in the field.

In particular, pregnant or nursing women, people traveling with children and people who are at higher-than-average risk of health problems may have special healthcare needs when they are away from home. The latter group includes people with diabetes, epilepsy, heart, liver or kidney disorders, skin conditions, or a history of splenectomy, as well as those who are HIV-positive or otherwise immunocompromised. If you are in any of these categories, seek advice from your doctor before you leave.

Sources of additional information about health risks in particular countries or regions and additional information on commonly encountered health problems are listed in Resources.

Why think about your health? Back home, you may be used to never giving a thought to your health except when you actually get sick. There are several good reasons for being more self-conscious about your health when you are on assignment:

- It is unpleasant to feel bad physically, and especially so when you are far from home and loved ones. Most of us are happier when we are healthy.

- When you are in the field, you may be exposed to risks you are not accustomed to. Infectious diseases such as malaria, dengue and typhus, parasites such as hookworms and the flatworms that cause schistosomiasis, food and water borne infections, the adverse effects of extreme climates on wound healing, and accidents all await the unwary aid worker.

- You are being sent to your assignment to do a job. From a purely rational point of view, your body is a machine and, like other machines, it is more efficient and more reliable if it is well maintained. If your body is in good condition, you can do your job better. You do not miss days at work and you work at maximum efficiency when you are at work.

    Conversely, if you are unhealthy, you miss time at work or you cannot pull your full load. In extreme cases, others on your work team may have to devote time or energy to taking care of you or may have to pick up work you should have done. If you do not maintain your health, you easily become a burden, an obstacle to the others on your team getting their own work done.

- Healthy people deal with stress better, and there is lots of stress in humanitarian work. Conversely, stress makes your body more susceptible to infection and can lead to behaviors that increase the likelihood of accidents.

- If you get sick or are hurt, you may not have access to the standard of medical care you would like to have. This is not just a matter of personal preference. Substandard medical care can be dangerous as well as ineffective. It may be hard to find a qualified doctor. The medicines that are available may be of inferior quality or out of date. And injections or transfusions carry a high risk of infection with HIV, hepatitis and other life-threatening illnesses.

Protecting your health in the field begins well before you leave for your assignment. We have discussed this topic at length in Chapter 1. If you have not read that section of the manual, read it now. It continues even after you return home from an assignment. Protecting your health from late-appearing effects of having been in the field will be discussed in Chapter 6. In this chapter, we focus on what you can do to protect your health while you are on your assignment. We will look at three complementary approaches to keeping yourself healthy.

1 You can prevent exposure to the viruses, bacteria, parasites and other environmental challenges that lead to illness in the first place.

2 You can keep your body strong so that you are less likely to succumb to illness if you are exposed.

3 If you do get sick or hurt, you can act to keep your illness or injuries from getting worse.

Preventing exposure to the environmental causes of illness

Many illnesses are caused by microorganisms, for example, bacteria, viruses and parasites, in the environment. There are four major ways that these microorganisms get to you.

- Contaminated water – for example, bacillary and viral diarrhea, amoebic dysentery, cholera, Hepatitis A, Hepatitis E, roundworms.

- Contaminated food – for example, bacillary and viral diarrhea, cholera, typhoid fever, brucellosis, Hepatitis A, Hepatitis E, tapeworm.

- Insects and ticks – for example, malaria, yellow fever, tick-borne encephalitis, Lyme Disease, plague, scabies, Tumbu fly boils, Chagas disease, leishmaniasis, sleeping sickness, dengue, river blindness.

- Direct person to person transmission, such as by sneezing, coughing, hand shaking, or sexual contact – for example, HIV/AIDS, Hepatitis B, Hepatitis C, meningococcal meningitis, tuberculosis, syphilis and other sexually transmitted diseases, Lassa fever.

The simplest way to prevent the diseases caused by these environmental sources is to keep yourself from being exposed to them in the first place.

Avoiding contaminated water

Contaminated water is a major source of disease in many parts of the world. You need clean water for drinking, brushing your teeth and rinsing dishes, cutlery and food preparation surfaces. Finding a source of clean water can be a challenge. Be skeptical of claims that the water is potable – for example, in a hotel or restaurant.

There are four ways to sterilize water: filtration, boiling, chemical disinfection and solar disinfection. Whichever method you choose, if the water is cloudy, let it stand to let the dirt settle out of it. You may want to filter it through several layers of cloth as well. Then proceed to the sterilization procedure.

Filtration
Filter the water using a commercially available ceramic filtering system. These are readily available at camping goods stores. Be sure to maintain the filter according to the manufacturer's instructions or it will become ineffective.

Boiling

Boil the water for three to five minutes. Add an additional minute for every thousand meters altitude above sea level. If you do not have cooking facilities, a small electric kettle will suffice. Let the water cool and stand for a few hours to improve the taste.

Disinfection

Add two drops of household bleach per liter of water. Use bleach that is 5–6 per cent chlorine and be sure there is no soap or other active ingredients in the brand you buy. If the water is cloudy, double the dose. Let the water stand for 30 minutes. At the end of the 30 minutes, it should still have a very faint chlorine odor. If not, add two more drops per liter of chlorine and again let it stand. To remove the odor, aerate the water by shaking it in a closed, previously sterilized container.

If you do not have a medicine dropper to measure out the chlorine, cut a 7 mm by 5 cm (1/4 inch by 2 inch) strip of cloth or paper. Lay the paper in the bowl of a spoon with about 1.2 cm (1/2 inch) hanging over the edge of the spoon. Pour some bleach in the spoon and carefully tip it. The drops that drip from the end of the paper or cloth will be about the right size.

Instead of chlorine, you can also use iodine: five drops of 2 per cent tincture of iodine per liter of water, if the water is clear and not turbid. You should not use water sterilized in this way for more than six weeks or if you have a thyroid condition.

Commercial water purifying tablets are also available; follow directions on the label.

Solar disinfection

After allowing the water to clarify by letting it stand for several hours, decant it into a clean clear or blue tinted – not tan or brown – glass or plastic vessel. A clean, loose-fitting cover will keep dust out, but is not essential. Place the vessel outdoors in full sunlight. Keep the container upright. Exposure to the sun for five hours should be sufficient to sterilize the water. In emergencies, two hours in full sunlight is sufficient to kill most germs. Even if the day is cloudy, but not heavily overcast or raining, solar disinfection works. Simply extend the time the vessel is exposed to light by an hour or two.

Once you have sterilized the water, store it in a covered, sterilized container. This can be the vessel used to boil it or chlorinate it or a previously cleaned and sterilized glass or earthenware jar. If you store it in plastic, it will pick up an odd taste. To sterilize a container, clean it; fill with a 0.1 per cent bleach solution (two drops of 5 per cent household bleach per liter of water; let it stand for twenty minutes; then empty it.

Retrieve the stored water by pouring or by a spout built into the storage vessel. Do *not* dip into the storage vessel – you will recontaminate the water.

On the road, you may want to take with you a supply of sterile drinking water from a trusted source. Hot drinks, such as coffee or tea, are probably safe. Water and beer and soft drinks from a bottle with a sealed metal top are probably safe, but sometimes bottles and caps are re-used, so look for signs the cap has been tampered with – for example, cap and bottle from different brands. Beware local products unless you know them to be from a reputable firm. Avoid ice in drinks. The alcohol in alcoholic drinks is not strong enough to sterilize the ice if the ice is contaminated. Avoid milk unless it has been boiled immediately before using.

Avoiding contaminated food

Few travelers escape at least a mildly upset stomach or mild diarrhea. These are usually self-limiting. Other more serious diseases, such as typhoid, amoebic dysentery, Hepatitis A and E, meningitis and cholera are also spread through contaminated food. Try to steer a course between being overly casual and being paranoid about food. The basic rule for food handling is: *cook it, peel it, clean it or forget it.*

■ Cooked vegetables and fruits are generally safe. Coffee and tea are generally safe, as long as the water used to make them has been brought to a boil. Boil milk for five minutes and let it cool. Keep it covered and cool.

■ You can peel fruits such as oranges and bananas without a utensil. With other fruits and vegetables that require a knife or other utensil to peel them, you may recontaminate them while peeling them. This is because the peeling utensil first touches the skin of the fruit, then the inside of the fruit or vegetable. Clean them before peeling.

First, clean off any gross dirt. Then soak them for 20 minutes in a 0.1 per cent bleach solution – two drops of 5 per cent household bleach per liter of water. Finally, rinse them with boiled, unchlorinated, water to get rid of the chlorine taste.

■ Do not allow cooked food to be contaminated by raw or uncooked food or by surfaces 'cleaned' with unclean water. Keep food preparation areas meticulously clean. Use soap and hot, chlorinated or boiled water. Rinse plates, cups, glasses, serving dishes and cutlery with a 0.1 per cent bleach solution – two drops of 5 per cent household bleach per liter of water – after washing and before putting them away. Use the same dilute bleach solution to rinse cutting boards and other surfaces that may come in contact with food after washing them with hot soap and water.

■ Protect food from flies and rodents. Cover it with a net or put it in a closed container or closed cupboard.

■ Be sure any household servants, especially those involved in food preparation and cleaning up, observe hand washing rules and do not cook or serve food when ill. Be sure they know and follow the rules above.

When you are eating in restaurants or at roadside stands or at someone else's house, wash your hands before eating and try to avoid, or clean, suspicious looking cutlery and glasses and crockery. Never share drinking vessels. If you are eating at someone else's house, try to identify safe foods and concentrate on them. Conversely, identify suspect foods and avoid them. If necessary, play with your food and pretend to eat without doing so. Or come up with strategies: excuse yourself as being a foreigner with a weak digestive system; or say the doctor has ordered you to avoid certain foods because of a specific health problem; or say it is against your religion to eat a certain food or share a drinking vessel; or say you are fasting for religious reasons.

Box 3   Eating out: what to eat and what not to eat

Avoid	Okay
Table sauces, which may be diluted with unsafe water.	Cooked foods that are still hot.
Salads, previously peeled or unpeeled fruits.	Hot coffee and tea.
Ice. Ice in alcoholic beverages remains unsafe. At the concentrations found in beer, wine, and hard liquor, alcohol does not sterilize the ice.	Food from freshly opened cans and sealed containers.
Milk and milk products such as ice cream and cheese.	Beer or soft drinks in bottles with intact caps. (But be sure the bottle has not been opened and reused. Look for caps that do not match the brand of the bottle or that are loose fitting or bent).
Uncooked vegetables and fruits.	
Cooked foods that have been allowed to cool.	
Local (unbottled) beers.	
Unbottled water.	
Rare meat.	
Egg unless cooked until the yolk is solid.	

Avoiding insect-borne diseases

Mosquitoes carry the germs that cause malaria, dengue, encephalitis and yellow fever; ticks the germs that cause tick-borne encephalitis, relapsing fever and Lyme Disease; fleas the germs that cause plague and typhus. Flies can transfer the germs that cause cholera, typhoid and other forms of dysentery from feces or contaminated food to a person. Tumbu flies cause skin lesions that look like boils. Other insect borne diseases include river blindness (black flies), Chagas disease ('kissing' bugs), leishmaniasis (sandflies), and sleeping sickness (tsetse flies). The simplest way to protect yourself from these diseases is to avoid contact with the insects.

- Cover as much of your skin as you can from just before sunset until after dawn. Wear long sleeves, long pants. Wear closed shoes when walking outside the home, not sandals or flip-flops. In addition to protecting your feet from insects, this will help avoid hookworm infections.

- Use insect repellent containing 20–35 per cent DEET. Higher concentrations are no more effective and may irritate the skin. Apply the repellent liberally to exposed skin and on hat brims, shirt collars and cuffs, pants cuffs and socks.

- Be sure your windows have adequate screens (6–7 wires per centimeter). If screens are not adequate, keep the windows closed and use an air conditioner, if possible. If not, use an aerosol spray in the bathroom and sleeping area before bedtime and keep windows closed from two hours before sunset until well after dawn.

- Use a mosquito net when you are sleeping. The net should be pre-soaked with permethrin, deltamethrin, lambdacyhalothrin, or another effective insect repellent. Resoak the net with permethrin or one of the other repellents every six months and after every washing. Be sure the net is roomy enough so that your feet or knees do not press against it, since mosquitoes can bite a limb that is pressed against the netting. Inspect the netting regularly for holes.

- After walking in the bush or woods, check your body carefully for ticks.

- Keep clothes clean and wash and change bed linens frequently. Dry them on a line, not on the ground where they can pick up insects that carry germs. This is especially important in tropical Africa and South America, where flies – Tumbu flies, putsi, mango flies, warble flies – can cause troublesome boils. Hot iron all clothes left outside to dry in those parts of the tropics where these insects are common.

- Keep your living quarters swept clean. Do not leave food on counters and clean up crumbs and scraps that fall to the floor. Clean toilets regularly and keep the kitchen especially clean. Keep the surroundings of your living quarters clear of standing water, which breeds mosquitoes, and high brush, which harbors snakes. Keep window screens in good repair. Use fly traps and insecticides to kill insects. Use poisons and traps to get rid of mice and rats.

Preventing person-to-person transmission of disease

Many diseases are transmitted directly from one person to another through sneezing, coughing, hand shaking or sexual contact – for example, HIV/AIDS, Hepatitis B, Hepatitis C, meningococcal meningitis, tuberculosis, syphilis and other sexually transmitted diseases, Lassa fever. Several steps help minimize the likelihood that you will 'catch' something from others:

- Wash your hands frequently – without being obsessive about it. Always wash them after using the toilet, before preparing food and before eating. Other times to wash are after touching possibly contaminated surfaces, after holding children, after handling money, after shaking hands and after touching animals, including household pets.

- When you wash your hands, use soap and hot water that you know is not contaminated or which has been sterilized. Rub your hands together vigorously to work up a good lather for at least 10–15 seconds; and rinse. Remember to remove jewelry before washing – germs can hide under a ring. Be sure to cover all surfaces of the hands and fingers, including the back of your hands and between your fingers. Use your own towel or paper towels or shake your hands dry. Turn off the faucet (tap) with a towel to avoid recontaminating your hands.

- Waterless, alcohol-based, hand scrubs or towelettes are an equally effective way of killing germs, unless your hands are heavily soiled with dirt. Rub your dry hands with the scrub for 20–30 seconds.

- Wash the rest of your body frequently. This is especially important in hot climates, where the heat and humidity create ideal conditions for germs to thrive. Remember that the water in the tub or shower may be contaminated. Let the water run briefly before getting in the shower and avoid getting it in your mouth.

- Cover your mouth when you sneeze or cough and insist that others do the same. If you have a cold or you are around anyone else who does, be especially diligent about washing your hands.

AIDS and Hepatitis B

AIDS and Hepatitis B, as well as a host of more treatable diseases, are spread through exchanges of body fluids during sex, through dirty needles used for injections and through contaminated blood used for transfusions.

Hepatitis B – which can lead to permanent liver damage and liver cancer – needs fewer virus particles to start infection than almost any other viral illness and in many cases the precise route of transmission can not be identified. An effective vaccine is available for Hepatitis B and as long as you keep your immunizations up to date, it should not be a problem.

AIDS is quite a different matter. AIDS is caused by the human immunodeficiency virus (HIV). The virus is found in the blood, semen, vaginal mucus and, at very low levels, in the saliva of those who are HIV-positive. You can only get it if virus from one of these fluids finds its way into your body. The most common routes are through sexual contact with someone who is HIV-positive, from a blood transfusion with contaminated blood, or from an injection using an inadequately sterilized needle previously used on an HIV-positive person. Other possible modes of transmission include lancets used for malaria smears, dental instruments, scalpels used in surgery, tattoo and ear-piercing needles and razor blades. HIV can also be spread from an HIV-positive mother to her child during birth or through breast milk. HIV is not spread through casual social contact. You can not get HIV from a toilet seat, from drinking from a cup shared by someone with HIV, from shaking hands with an HIV-positive person, from being in a room where an HIV-positive person has sneezed, or from swimming in the same pool as an HIV-positive person, or from a kiss on the cheek.

What you need to do to protect yourself:

- Unless you are in a long-term monogamous relationship with someone known to be HIV negative, always use a condom. Be aware that after a person is infected with HIV, there is a 'window period' during which they still test negative but are nevertheless infectious to others. Use a condom even if you are using other modes of contraception. Diaphragms, birth control pills and other forms of birth control may prevent pregnancy but they do not prevent transmission of the AIDS virus.

- Avoid casual sex. In some areas of the world, more than 25 per cent of the population and over 75 per cent of sex workers are HIV-positive. Even with condoms, you place yourself at risk. It has been estimated that condoms fail up to 10–20 per cent of the time due to breakage, slippage or carelessness.

- Sores and ulcerations in the genital area make it easier for the AIDS virus to enter your body. Have them treated promptly and avoid sex altogether until they heal.

- Blood supplies in many poorer countries are often inadequately tested. If you are in a country without good screening of donors and testing of blood supplies, avoid transfusions save in the most desperately urgent life-threatening situations. Only accept blood that has been tested for HIV immediately before you are to receive it. You may accept a blood donation from a donor who you know to be free of HIV (and whose life style you trust; if they have become infected in the last two or three months, they may still test negative). Also avoid locally produced gamma globulin or other blood-derived products.

In almost all situations, treatment with intravenous fluids or a plasma substitute can be used to buy time until you can get to a place where safe transfusions are available. If your assignment requires you to travel extensively by car in remote areas or by light airplane, consider taking an AIDS and Hepatitis B protection kit (an IV-giving set and IV fluid) and get instructions in how to use it. The Blood Care Foundation in England (http://www.bloodcare. org.uk) claims to get safe blood to almost any location in the world within 24 hours, but you have to be a member to be eligible for this service. Both long-term and short-term memberships are available.

Avoid situations that may create the need for a transfusion or injection. This reemphasizes the importance of avoiding motor vehicle accidents. Wearing a seat belt, regardless of whether you are in the front seat or the back seat, even for short rides, is probably the most important health precaution you can take. Make sure any vehicle you ride is in good repair – especially check the brakes and the tires. If you are on a motorbike or motorcycle, wear a helmet. Avoid driving when you are tired or when you are taking medications that make you drowsy. Take your time. And never mix driving and drinking.

■ Avoid dirty needles, syringes, and lancets. In many areas of the world, poorly trained health workers readily offer injections for even mild and self-limiting conditions. Turn down such recommendations, unless they are from a well-trained professional. Ask for oral medications rather than preparations administered by injection. In any case, do not accept an injection except in a health facility where you know they use sterile, disposable needles and syringes. In any other situation, provide your own sterile needle and syringe, and make sure that the nurse uses the equipment you provide. If you will be in a malarial area, provide your own lancet for a malaria smear. Delay any non-urgent surgery or dentistry until you visit or return home.

Preventing exposure to miscellaneous other health problems

Several other precautions which can help avoid some diseases merit attention.

Swimming

The parasites that cause schistosomiasis (bilharzia) are found in fresh water rivers and lakes. In areas where schistosomiasis is common, avoid swimming in fresh water ponds or rivers. In sub-Saharan Africa, the greatest risk is at the southern end of Lake Malawi, where infection rates are about 80 per cent of swimmers.

With salt water bays and oceans, the greatest problem is that raw sewage from towns may be discharged directly into the water, without treatment. Avoid swimming on beaches near cities or where there are obvious sources of pollution, especially if there is a known cholera outbreak.

Sun, heat, and cold

In hot climates you risk heat exhaustion and sun stroke as well as sun burn. Wear loose-fitting clothes. Drink plenty of fluids. Stay in the shade during the middle part of the day, from about 10:00 am to 3:00 pm. If you must go out in the sun, use a sunscreen with a rating of SPF 30 and wear a hat with a brim.

In colder climates, wear several layers of clothes rather than a single bulky layer. That way you can remove a layer if you start to get hot. In colder areas, the greatest danger is getting wet. Wetness, whether from precipitation or from your own sweat, increases the rate of loss of heat from your body and reduces the insulating efficiency of most fabrics. However, wool remains warm even when wet. In wet weather, wear a waterproof layer over your clothes: raincoat or poncho or waterproof anorak, hat, and boots.

Alcohol

The biggest health problem associated with drinking is that too much alcohol makes you forget all of the other precautions you should be taking with regard to your health.

Drinking and driving are not compatible. Even small amounts of alcohol interfere with coordination and slow your responses. In addition to injuries from the car accident itself, accidents often lead to loss of blood, and if you require a transfusion to replace blood, you run a very serious risk of HIV infection. Whenever you go out, make sure someone agrees to be the 'designated driver' and stays away from alcohol altogether. If you cannot do that, take a taxi.

Drinking also lowers your inhibitions about casual sex and undermines your intentions of engaging in 'safe sex'. Where HIV is common, that can be fatal. Drink, if you wish, but drink in moderation.

Driving

Motor vehicle accidents are the most common causes of death and injury to staff of humanitarian projects. Safety in cars is discussed above, on pages 35–38. At the risk of repetition, wear your seatbelt at all times, whether you are the driver or a passenger. Slow down: speed kills. And if someone else is driving, ask your driver to slow down, if necessary.

Keeping your defenses up: acting to keep your immune system strong

We are used to describing exposure to disease-causing organisms – bacteria, viruses, amoeba, parasites – as the 'cause' of an illness. For example, we say we got a cold because we were 'exposed' to someone who had the virus that causes colds. But in fact, we are exposed to disease-causing organisms every day, both on assignment and at home, yet we usually do not get sick. The *immediate cause* of our getting sick is often some factor that has weakened our immune system, such as being 'run down' or 'stressed out' or 'over-tired'. The enemy is always at the gates. We succumb when we let down our defenses.

One of the easiest, and most pleasant, ways of keeping healthy is to act to maintain your defenses. Here's how.

Nutrition and hydration

Poor nutrition may make you more likely to get an infectious disease. When you are traveling away from home, it can be hard to maintain your usual patterns of eating. Familiar foods may not be available and the foods that are available may seem strange. Your work schedule may make the eating schedule you have had in the past impossible. Several principles will help you get back on track.

- Do not eat on the run – sit down and take your time to eat to digest your food properly. Try to eat regularly. It is better for your health to eat three to five moderately sized meals a day than to snack all day and then eat one big meal at the end of the day. Do not forget breakfast: A substantial meal at the start of the day will give you the energy you need to work efficiently.

- Eat in moderation. If you find yourself gaining weight, eat a little less each day – one cookie a day adds up to a couple of pounds in a month – and exercise a little more. If you are losing weight, do not cut back on the exercise – just eat a bit more.

■ Eat a balanced diet. Your body needs protein, fat and carbohydrate, as well as various minerals and vitamins. Most of the world's staple foods – for example, rice, corn, wheat, cassava – contain protein, but all these vegetable proteins are 'incomplete'. Proteins are made up of more than twenty different 'amino acids', but all vegetable proteins lack at least one type of amino acid your body needs. Since different kinds of vegetable proteins lack different amino acids, by mixing different vegetable sources of protein together you can get all of the essential amino acids. Divide vegetable foods into three groups: grasses, for example, wheat, corn, rice; legumes, for example, beans, lentils, peas; and nuts, including peanuts or groundnuts. If you mix foods from any two groups together at the same meal, you will get a 'complete' protein. Try rice and beans or peanut butter and wheat bread. Or add a small amount of animal-based protein, such as milk, cheese, eggs, poultry, fish, or meat, to any vegetable-source of protein – for example, meat or fish sauce on pasta, milk with cereal.

Try to keep fat consumption down to 30 per cent of your caloric intake. Vegetable fats – for example, corn oil, olive oil, soy oil – are generally better for your heart than animal fats. The exceptions are cocoa oil and palm oil, which are like animal fats in their effects. And look out for 'empty calories' – carbohydrate-rich foods that fill you up but do not meet your other nutritional needs.

One way of ensuring that you get the minerals and vitamins you need is to 'mix colors' – green, orange, yellow and red vegetables complement each other. If you mix them up, you will get what you need. There is lots of evidence that a diet rich in fruits and vegetables protects you against many illnesses, but remember to clean them properly to eliminate germs from their skins. If you find it hard to eat a lot of vegetables and fruits, you may want to take a vitamin and mineral supplement.

■ Do not eat as a way of dealing with stress. If you find you are doing so, see Chapter 4. Limit the junk food. One recent study found that humanitarian workers who ate more snack food reported more adverse symptoms of stress. There is no way to eat a lot of junk food without loading up on fat and salt. If you are hungry during the day, try some fruit or a handful of nuts.

■ Drink enough water. You should drink enough to urinate at least twice a day. It may be more difficult to be sure that you will be able to find safe water to drink when you are on the road, so carry a canteen or bottled water when you travel.

Sleep, rest and relaxation

Do not let yourself get run down. Getting enough rest helps keep your body strong. It also makes it less likely that you will get into an accident.

Try to get enough sleep. Different people need different amounts of sleep, but most adults need about seven to eight hours a night at least six days a week. If you have to drag yourself out of bed in the morning or if you have trouble staying awake later in the day, you are getting too little sleep for your body. If you have trouble falling asleep or staying asleep or if you find yourself waking up at the crack of dawn, try to maintain a regular sleep schedule. Go to bed at the same time every night. Avoid beverages or foods containing caffeine – coffee, tea, cola drinks, chocolate – late in the afternoon or evening and avoid alcohol or heavy meals just before bed. Take regular rest breaks at work and take off at least one whole day a week, save in emergencies. Take a longer break – at least a long weekend – at least once a month.

Exercise

Regular physical activity four to seven days a week reduces the risk of developing some of the leading causes of illness and death. Regular physical activity reduces the rate of respiratory infections, reduces the risk of dying from heart disease, reduces the risk of developing diabetes, reduces the risk of developing high blood pressure and helps reduce blood pressure in people who already have high blood pressure, reduces the risk of developing colon cancer and possibly prostate, breast, lung, testicular and uterine cancer. Regular exercise also helps control weight, helps maintain healthy muscles, bones and joints, increases the capacity to recover from strenuous work and promotes psychological well-being.

Your work assignment, itself, may provide at least some of the exercise you need. If your job requires that you be on your feet, doing a lot of walking, stretching or lifting, your need for additional exercise will, of course, be less than if you have a sedentary, desk job. One way or another, however, you should try to get three different kinds of exercise on a regular basis:

- Aerobic exercise – the kind of exercise that makes you breathe faster and makes your heart rate get faster – such as jogging, running, swimming (but first see p. 60), playing volleyball, or dancing. Aim for three or four 30-minute sessions a week.

- Flexibility building exercise – the kind of exercise that stretch your muscles – such as stretching or yoga. Try to do every day.

- Weight bearing (strength) exercise – the kind of exercise that builds muscles – such as weight lifting, walking or simple gymnastic exercises. Three sessions a week is fine.

Maintaining malaria prophylaxis and other immunizations

In many poorer nations of the world, malaria is the most serious and most important threat to your health that you face. It causes much chronic bad health and an estimated two million deaths every year. Drug-resistant strains of the organism that causes malaria have emerged in many areas, so it is especially important to try not to get malaria in the first place.

Malaria prophylaxis begins before you leave for your assignment, continues during your assignment and then goes on for a while after the end of your assignment. Take the prophylactic medication prescribed for you by your doctor religiously. Avoid changing to a different regimen unless there is a compelling reason. Do not miss doses. Remember to take your pills with you when you travel and on holiday. Even if the holiday is 'back home' or to some other area where malaria is not a problem, maintaining a continuously high level of the medication in your blood is necessary for immunization.

There are many myths about malaria.

You accommodate to a malarial environment after a while and no longer need the pills

False. Think about the millions of people a year who live their whole lives in malarial environments – lives that are shorter because far from adapting to it they die of it. It takes at least 10 years of continuous exposure to malaria to become semi-immune.

The prophylactic regimens do not really work

False. There is plenty of evidence that they do prevent malaria and that when they fail to prevent it, they make it milder.

If you are taking anti-malaria medications, if you do get malaria there will not be anything left to treat it with

False. There are several other medications still left to treat it.

Garlic, vitamin B, yeast or other substances are just as good as the prescription medications

False. There is no evidence that any of the former work at all.

The *true* answer to the question of how to prevent malaria is very simple. It has two parts:

1 Choose a prophylactic medication regimen before you leave for your assignment, with the aid of your doctor. Then follow it. Note that prophylactic medication regimens may require modification for children, pregnant or breast-feeding women, those with epilepsy, liver or kidney problems and those with a history of splenectomy. Discuss your individual needs with your doctor.

2 Take all possible precautions to prevent getting bitten by mosquitoes: mosquito nets, use of insect repellents, long sleeves and long pants, screens on windows and doors, etc. (see above).

Other infectious diseases are also a threat. You should have received all of your immunizations before leaving for your assignment, but remember that periodic booster shots are needed for most immunizations. If it is more than two years since your last shots, check Box 4.

Box 4	**Re-immunization schedule**

Disease	Booster shot interval
Diphtheria and tetanus	10 years
Hepatitis A	10 years
Japanese B encephalitis	3 years
Meningitis	3 years
Polio	10 years
Rabies	2–3 years
Typhoid	3 years
Yellow fever	10 years

Hepatitis B: Two to four months after your initial series of shots, have your immunity level checked. Non-immunocompromised patients who have developed adequate immunity will not need a booster for at least 10 to 15 years.

Stress

When you are 'stressed out', your immune system and other systems involved in keeping you healthy do not function as effectively as they might and your resistance to getting sick falls. For example, one study found that wounds took longer to heal in women who were stressed by their role as caretaker for a family member with Alzheimer's disease. Other studies have found that people who are under more stress are more likely to catch colds and the flu and to have more severe symptoms after they fall ill. Even the response of the body's immune system to a flu vaccine has been found to be affected by their emotional state. Stress is a topic often poorly understood by aid workers and merits an extended discussion. It is discussed in detail in Chapter 4.

Keeping things from getting worse

It is almost inevitable that, sooner or later, you will get sick. What you do next may determine whether you get better quickly or get really sick.

Medical care, injections, transfusions and medicines

We have already discussed many of the problems you may encounter in getting adequate medical care abroad, but remember that sub-standard medical care may actually be a cause of sickness or death. It may be hard to find a qualified doctor in an emergency, it is better to be prepared. As soon as you get to your assignment, try to find out about qualified healthcare facilities and practitioners in the area. Ask your team members, supervisor or your embassy. Arrange to have any non-urgent surgery or dentistry done when you visit or return home.

At the risk of repetition, if you are in a country without good screening of blood donors and testing of blood supplies, avoid transfusions save in the most urgent life-threatening situations (See p. 59). Avoid situations that may create the need for a transfusion. If your assignment requires you to travel extensively by car in remote areas or by light airplane, consider taking an AIDS and Hepatitis B protection kit, and get instructions in how to use it.

Repetition again: dirty needles, syringes and lancets may be sources of life-threatening diseases (see p. 60). Ask for oral medications rather than preparations administered by injection. Never accept an injection except in a health facility where you know they use sterile, disposable needles and syringes. In any other situation, provide your own sterile needle and syringe and your own lancet for a malaria smear and ascertain that the nurse uses the equipment you provide.

Locally available medicines may be out of date or produced or stored under sub-standard conditions, or, in the case of 'traditional' remedies, untested, possibly useless and possibly dangerous. Just because a medication is 'natural' or 'traditional' does not mean it cannot cause serious side effects. Especially avoid locally produced gamma globulin or other blood-derived products. Bring the medications you use on a regular basis from home or arrange to have them sent out to you.

Fevers

Most fevers are mild and self limiting. Rest and drinking plenty of fluids will get you through it. If you are really uncomfortable, try acetaminophen – paracetamol, Tylenol, etc.; ibuprofen – Advil, Motrin, Nurofen, etc.; or aspirin every four hours. Avoid aspirin in children under 16.

Take seriously any high fever, over 39°C or 102°F, or any mild fever that lasts more than three days. Fever may be a sign of any of several serious illnesses, including malaria, typhoid, dengue, and hepatitis, schistosomiasis, typhus, sleeping sickness, meningitis, dysentery and Lassa fever. Finding out what diseases are common in the area in which you work may reassure you about some of the possibilities, but several of these can be *rapidly fatal* unless treated promptly. See a qualified health professional fast.

In malarial areas, assume *any* fever to be malaria until proven otherwise. Symptoms of malaria vary. The fever may be very high but it may not be. Chills, headache, sweats, pain in the joints and vomiting or diarrhea may precede or accompany the fever. If you are in a malarial area see a qualified health worker immediately and get a blood smear. (Remember to take your own sterile lancet). If you are in a remote area where no *reliable* medical assistance will be available for more than 24 hours and you suspect you have malaria, many doctors recommend that you begin treating yourself. Even if you have had a blood smear done and the smear is negative, begin self-treatment if symptoms persist. Get expert advice on self treatment ahead of time. There are several medication regimens commonly used, but the existence of resistant strains of malarial makes choosing the right one for the area you are traveling in essential. If you will be going to an area with a high malaria risk and unreliable treatment, carry the appropriate anti-malarial tablets with you.

Diarrhea

Diarrhea caused by bacteria, viruses, amoeba or other parasites is an almost universal experience for those spending extended time in areas outside of North America, Western Europe, Australia and New Zealand. Some people seem more resistant than others and many expatriates develop resistance to intestinal upsets after living abroad for a year or two. If there is blood in the stools, it is known as dysentery. It may or may not be accompanied by fever or other symptoms.

While diarrhea is often mild and self-limiting, it may be a sign of a serious illness. Repeated bowel infections can cause the lining of the small intestine to be less efficient in absorbing food, which can lead to malnutrition even though you are eating properly. Even mild diarrhea, if sustained, can cause dehydration – which can lead to imbalances of salt and minerals in the body and occasionally be life threatening.

Regardless of the cause, it is essential to replace lost body fluid. Begin oral rehydration at the slightest sign of illness. Drink plenty of any non-alcoholic and non-milk based drinks – for example, Coke, Sprite, weak tea or light soup. If you use a carbonated drink, shake it to remove most of the bubbles first.

You can also buy packets of commercially available oral rehydration salts and mix them with water, following the instructions on the label. The World Health Organization currently recommends a formulation that contains 2.6 g sodium chloride, 2.9 g trisodium citrate, 1.5 g potassium chloride and 13.5 g glucose in a liter of water). In an emergency, you can make your own rehydration fluid. If you cannot get all of the ingredients to make up the currently recommended WHO formula, dissolving six level teaspoons sugar and one level teaspoon salt in one liter of safe drinking water is better than trying to replace fluids with water alone. If possible, add some mashed ripe bananas – for potassium – and some orange, lemon or grapefruit juice – for taste.

If your symptoms are relatively mild and do not interfere with ordinary activities and you feel generally okay, just keep up your fluid intake and eat a light diet until the symptoms disappear. If your symptoms are severe enough to interfere with your ordinary activities but you feel reasonably well and have no fever and no blood in your stool, many doctors will recommend that you take loperamide (Imodium), two 2 mg tablets followed by one tablet every four to six hours and/or ciprofloxacin (Cipro), two 250 mg tablets a day, until the diarrhea ceases. (Cipro should be accompanied by plenty of fluids and should not be taken by children under age sixteen or by women who are pregnant or breast feedings). If you feel unwell or have a fever, you may continue the Cipro (two 250 mg tablets a day) for five to seven days. Remember to keep up your fluid intake.

If you have blood or mucus in your stool and/or fever, see a doctor and get a stool test. There are many possible diagnoses, including bacterial dysentery (usually caused by Shigella), amoebic dysentery, giardiasis, schistosomiasis, typhoid fever and cholera. Proper treatment depends on identifying the organism. If you are in a remote area and there will be a delay before you can see the doctor, take Cipro, as suggested above.

Cuts and bruises

In hot, humid climates, cuts, bruises, blisters and other breaks in the skin easily get infected. Clean all injuries well. Use an antibiotic cream and keep the injury covered with a light dressing. Change the dressing frequently until the skin has healed. A brief first aid manual can be found in the Resources section.

CHAPTER 4
Managing stress

Myths about stress and humanitarian workers

The 'ARC' model
    Anticipate the stresses of humanitarian work
    Reduce the stresses of humanitarian work
    Cope with the stresses of humanitarian work

Spiritual Resources for Humanitarian workers

Myths about stress and humanitarian workers

Many humanitarian workers will see the title of this chapter and react with scorn or lack of interest.

'If you can't stand the heat, get out of the kitchen.' We who choose to work in the humanitarian field are tough and can withstand everything that our jobs throw at us. Fact: Although many humanitarian workers withstand the rigors of their work without adverse effects, many others do not. One recent study found that as many as one-third of recently returned expatriate staff showed significant signs of emotional distress. Similar levels of distress have been reported in national staff of humanitarian organizations. Both anecdotal reports and empirical studies have abundantly documented the negative emotional consequences of exposure to these stressors on various groups of humanitarian workers. These adverse consequences may include post-traumatic stress syndromes – resulting from direct exposure to or witnessing traumatizing experiences; 'vicarious' or 'secondary' traumatization – resulting from repeated exposure to the stories of and witnessing the suffering of direct victims of trauma; burnout; depression; pathological grief reactions; anxiety; 'over-involvement' or 'over-identification' with beneficiary populations or, conversely, callousness and apathy towards beneficiaries; self destructive behaviors such as excessive drinking or dangerous driving; and interpersonal conflict with co-workers or with family members.

'If you go out in the rain, you expect to get wet.' Everyone knows that there are risks in humanitarian work. We have to do the work despite those risks.

Fact: Although a high level of stress is inevitable in humanitarian work, many sources of stress can be eliminated or reduced. The effects of stress on individual staff members can also be reduced by actions undertaken by the individual staff members, by managers and supervisors, or by the humanitarian agency as a whole.

The whole point of humanitarian work is that there are people in need and *we* are here to help *them*. If we can't put their desperate needs ahead of our own relatively minor concerns, we are in the wrong business.

Fact: Stress and burnout have an adverse impact on the ability of the humanitarian worker to provide services to recipient groups as well as causing distress to the worker him or herself. Workers suffering from the effects of stress are likely to be less efficient and less effective in carrying out their assigned tanks. They are more likely to have accidents or become ill. They become poor decision makers and they may behave in ways that place themselves or other members of the team at risk or disrupt the effective functioning of the team. Staff members suffering from the effects of stress are not in a good position to make decisions about sensitive issues such as security. At stake is not only their own safety but that of others. 'Stressed-out workers make stupid decisions', commented the Safety and Security Coordinator of a large aid agency.

The bottom line is very simple: *It is impossible to take care of others for more than a short period of time if you do not take care of yourself.*

The 'ARC' model

In the remainder of this chapter we will present the 'ARC' model for responding to stress. The model reminds you to try to:

- *Anticipate* stress: Understand the phenomenon of stress, identify the specific stressors you will face as a humanitarian worker and learn to recognize signs of stress in yourself and your fellow workers. This creates opportunities to lessen potential sources of stress and to cope better with those that remain.

- *Reduce* or eliminate potential sources of stress. Learn what your agency, your team and you yourself can do to reduce or eliminate stressors. The effects of stress are cumulative. Even if you cannot eliminate all sources of stress, every source of stress you do eliminate or weaken reduces the overall load on you.

- *Cope* better with the stresses you cannot eliminate. Stress may be inevitable, but how you understand stress and how you respond to it play a major role in determining its long term effect on you.

Anticipate the stresses of humanitarian work

To understand stress, it is useful to make a distinction between stressful events (stressors), the physiological, behavioral, and psychological effects of the stressor on the individual (stress) and the behaviors, thoughts and feelings the individual uses to deal with the stressor and so reduce the stress (coping).

Stressors

Stressors range from the minor hassles of everyday life – for example, waiting in a long line to renew your passport – to more unusual but still relatively minor events – for example, being attacked verbally by someone you are trying to help or a conflict with a fellow team member or getting in a minor car accident – to more severe and possibly dangerous events – for example, coming up to an unexpected roadblock or coming under military attack. Even 'good' events – for example, getting married or getting promoted – can be stressful.

Most stressors are obvious, but some chronic sources of stress are less so. For example, national staff working for an international NGO may feel resentment stemming from their lesser pay and benefits and from their, often correct, feelings that the agency does not consult with them about programs and policies and has less concern with their safety and well-being than it has for that of expatriates. Such feelings create chronic stress in the local staff member but may be invisible to the expatriates. *In general, the effect of stressors is cumulative – many minor stressors can create as much stress in an individual as a few larger stressors.* One particular type of stressor deserves particular attention: 'traumatic stress' or 'critical incident' stress. This is the kind of stress that occurs when your life is threatened or you are threatened with severe bodily harm, or when you witness someone else's life taken, or someone else threatened with grave harm, and you experience feelings of horror, terror, rage and helplessness. Such extreme stressors are processed by our bodies and minds in a way that is distinct from the way other stressors – even serious ones – are processed. In general, an event that is stressful to one person may be only a minor challenge to another, but traumatic stressors are stressful for almost everyone. You may even experience high levels of stress simply from constant exposure to the suffering of the direct victims of traumatic events or from constantly hearing their terrible stories.

Stress

Your physiological, behavioral and emotional response to a stressful situation is called 'stress'. In response to a stressor, you mobilize cognitive, emotional, spiritual and physical energy to evaluate and respond to the threat. There is nothing intrinsically bad about stress. It is an adaptive response to a challenge in the external world and especially to potentially threatening situations. But chronic stress or stress that exceeds your ability to respond effectively, or that leads to maladaptive responses, is more problematic.

Coping
There are two basic strategies for responding to external challenges.

1 You can try to do something about the source of stress; i.e., you can try to make changes in yourself or your surroundings to eliminate or lessen the challenge or danger created by the stressor. This is a 'task-centered' response.

2 You can try to protect yourself from the unpleasant feelings stress creates in you. For example, you can do something to distract yourself from the problem – go to a movie; or do something to express your feelings – get angry; or do something to directly reduce the unpleasant feelings elicited by the stress – do a relaxation exercise. These are 'defensive' or 'emotion-centered' responses. In general, if it is possible to do something about the stressor, task-oriented coping is likely to be more successful at reducing stress. But sometimes there is little or nothing you can do to affect the stressor and effective use of the defensive strategies is more helpful.

The burden of stress
Even successful coping drains emotional and physical energy. When you first become aware of a source of stress, your resources for dealing with it are mobilized. You become emotionally aroused, alert and determined to respond. Stress may also arouse less desirable responses, such as feelings of anxiety or physiological distress such as headaches or muscular tension or gastrointestinal disturbances. If the stressor persists, you must continue to use mental energy to try to deal with it and maintain equilibrium in your life. Over time, your adaptive resources may become depleted. Your ability to deal with new stressors is diminished. You may feel exhausted, overwhelmed, stressed out and even your ability to carry out tasks that are normally non-stressful for you may be impaired. Feelings of emotional exhaustion appear. 'Stress' has turned into distress.

In the case of traumatic stress, the effects may be even more far reaching. Nightmares, flashbacks, a chronic state of physiological arousal, feelings of emotional numbness, lethargy, depression, irritability, increased frequency of interpersonal conflict and generalized anxiety may appear, along with a variety of psychosomatic illnesses. These symptoms may be long-lasting and disabling.

The stresses of humanitarian work
The stresses you are likely to experience as a humanitarian worker vary from assignment to assignment, but they may include any or all of the following.

■ Physically demanding and/or unpleasant working conditions; excessive work load, long hours and chronic fatigue; lack of privacy and personal space.

■ Separation from family and/or concerns about family well-being and/or loneliness.

- Constant exposure to danger, chronic fear, chronic uncertainty; facing the possibility, or experience, of repeated evacuations.

- Lack of adequate resources, personnel, time, logistical support or skills to do the job expected of you.

- Excessive bureaucratic demands or lack of supportive leadership and recognition from the employing agency, or employment practices that are perceived by staff as unclear or unfair.

- Interpersonal conflict among team members who are forced into close and prolonged proximity and interdependence.

- Sexual harassment or unwanted sexual advances from a team member or supervisor; negative attitudes or overly-critical behaviors by supervisors or managers.

- Repeated exposure to tales of traumatization and personal tragedy or to gruesome scenes, or to events and stories that trigger personally traumatic memories from the past.

- Direct exposure to traumatizing experiences: threats to your life or physical integrity or witnessing threats to others.

- A sense of helplessness or futility in the face of overwhelming need; anguish resulting from the need to triage; moral or ethical dilemmas – for example, having to negotiate with perpetrators of human rights abuses; having to maintain neutrality in politically polarized situations; guilt over access to food, shelter and other resources the beneficiary population does not have.

- Exposure to anger and apparent lack of gratitude from some among the beneficiary population.

- Experience of 'culture shock' – the strain of working in a culturally unfamiliar environment.

The signs of chronic stress and burnout

How do you know if you are experiencing the negative effects of chronic stress? Stress appears in many forms, not all of them immediately recognizable as stress.

- *Pay attention to your body.* For some people, moods come out in the form of physical complaints. Are you experiencing rapid heartbeat, stomach pains, tightness in the chest, trembling, feeling tired all the time, headaches and other aches and pains? Are you suffering from chronic colds? Are you having sleep problems – insomnia or excessive sleeping or nightmares?

- *Pay attention to your mind.* Are you having difficulty concentrating, difficulty remembering? Are you finding that you are more 'disorganized' than usual, feeling overwhelmed or fearful, thinking 'obsessively' about the same things over and over again, having trouble making decisions?

- *Pay attention to your personal life and your emotions.* Are you more irritable than you used to be? Feeling 'on edge' all the time? Arguing more with friends or co-workers or family members? Over-reacting to the failings of others? Losing your sense of humor? Feeling depressed or trapped? Wanting to withdraw from others? Are you constantly feeling angry or sad or fearful or hopeless or longing for a 'safe haven'?

- *Pay attention to your behavior.* Are you engaging in risky behaviors – for example, disregarding agency safety and security guidelines, drinking too much, smoking too much, using illegal drugs, being promiscuous, or driving recklessly. Are you going places or doing things that you would have previously thought were reckless? Are you withdrawing from friends or becoming more reluctant to participate in group activities? Are you late or absent from work too much? Are you neglecting taking care of yourself? Are you feeling abandoned or isolated? Are you having mood swings?

- *Pay attention to your spiritual/philosophical feelings.* Are you feeling disillusioned or 'angry at God'? Does the universe seem to make no sense to you? Do you feel feelings of 'emptiness'? Are you questioning the choices you have made in your life?

- *Pay attention to the life of your team.* You may see signs of stress in other members of the team. There may also be signs that the team as a whole is in distress. Look out for the formation of 'cliques', frequent bickering or conflict, lack of initiative or follow-through on the part of team members, growing inefficiency and reduced work output, scapegoating of an individual, or a high rate of job turnover.

Over time, the effects of chronic stress may lead to 'burnout'. Imperceptibly your attitude towards your work, your colleagues and the people you are supposedly helping changes. You find little pleasure in your work. You begin to feel ineffective, but somehow you cannot get up the energy to make the changes that would make you more effective. You may feel cynical about your work and engage in excessive 'black humor' about the recipients. You become more casual about being late or calling in 'sick'. You may feel bitter or cynical or 'jaded'. You may develop grandiose beliefs about your own importance to the job – for example, engage in heroic but reckless behaviors, ostensibly in the interests of helping others – or neglect your own safety and your own physical needs – for example, for breaks or for sleep – or come to mistrust or disparage co-workers or supervisors – as if they are not pulling their weight on the job. You may drink too much coffee or smoke too many cigarettes or drink too much alcohol.

To check on your own chronic stress and burnout level, complete the stress and burnout checklist in Box 5.

Signs of post-traumatic stress and secondary traumatization

Events that involve actual or threatened death or severe injury to yourself or to others and that are accompanied by intense fear, helplessness or horror, are called

Box 5	Stress and burnout checklist	Never (score 1)	Sometimes (score 20)	Often (score 3)
1	I feel tense and nervous			
2	I have physical aches and pains			
3	I am always tired, physically and mentally			
4	The smallest noise makes me jump			
5	My work no longer interests me			
6	I act impulsively and take a lot of risks			
7	I cannot get distressing events out of my mind			
8	I am sad and feel like crying			
9	I am less efficient than I used to be			
10	I have trouble planning and thinking clearly			
11	I have difficulty in sleeping			
12	Doing even routine things is an effort			
13	I am cynical and very critical			
14	I have bad dreams or nightmares			
15	I am irritable; minor inconveniences or demands annoy me a lot			

Add up your total score and interpret it according to the following guidelines:

Score 15–20   Your state of stress is normal, given your working conditions.

Score 21–30   You may be suffering from stress and should take it easy.

Score 31–45   You may be under severe stress. Ask for help from someone close to you and/or from your supervisor or manager or contact your doctor.

'traumatic experiences' or 'critical incidents' and the reactions to them are called 'post-traumatic stress reactions'.

Humanitarian workers are not infrequently exposed to such events. Especially if you are working in a context in which conflict is ongoing – for example, civil conflict, political repression, war refugee camps – you may yourself be a target of violence. Contact with survivors and providing advice and support to the local population may be seen as a threat to the state, to one or the other side in the conflict, or to powerful forces in the refugee camp. You may face threats to your life, real or threatened assault – individual or military, kidnapping or being taken hostage, detention or arrest, roadblocks manned by armed drunken teenagers. To make matters worse, in some situations, it may be hard to evoke the law for your own protection, because the police or the army is 'part of the problem'.

Even in more stable, non-conflict situations, you may be exposed to harrowing experiences, such as the death of a colleague in the line of work, deaths among those being assisted, or personal encounters with violence or 'atrocities'. The result may be a heightened sense of powerlessness, anger, fear and anxiety, and a pre-occupation with your own safety. You may experience feelings of betrayal and loss, of vulnerability, of loss in a belief in an orderly or just world.

Not only those who are directly involved in field operations as humanitarian workers are at risk of negative emotional effects from constant exposure to the sufferings of others. Human rights workers, journalists covering humanitarian emergencies, administrators of relief efforts and other office workers who are in close contact with workers in the field may also experience severe symptoms of stress.

If you have been directly exposed to terrifying or horrendous experiences, in the first hours or first few days after a traumatic event, you may experience a variety of emotional reactions. You may feel stunned, dazed, confused, apathetic or superficially calm. You may continue to experience intense feelings of fear, accompanied by physiological arousal – for example, heart pounding, muscle tension, muscular pains, gastrointestinal disturbances. You may show an exaggerated startle response, inability to relax, inability to make decisions, or have feelings of abandonment or anxiety about separation from loved ones, or a loss of a sense of safety. You may blame yourself or feel shame at having survived when others did not, or be pre-occupied with thoughts about the events and ruminations over your own behavior. You may flip back and forth between sudden anger and aggressiveness and apathy and lack of energy and inability to mobilize yourself. *Note. There is no one 'right' way to respond to traumatic incidents. You may shift from one kind of response to another or you may not show any evident response at all.*

For most people, these initial symptoms gradually subside over the days and weeks that follow, but for many others significant signs of distress persist for many weeks or months after the distressing experience (see Box 6, Signs of traumatic stress). Different people respond differently to traumatic events, depending on such factors as their actual experience, their previous experience of traumatic events and their typical ways of coping with trouble. For some people, the symptoms or trauma fade relatively quickly; for others they persist. For some people, 'going through the fire' may actually strengthen them and enhance their ability to cope and to deal with life joyously; for many others, the events produce distressing long-term symptoms. On occasion, symptoms may not appear until some months after the actual horrendous events. There is nothing wrong with you if you show a different pattern of response or if you do not have any of these responses.

Box 6   **Signs of traumatic stress**

■ Chronic depression, grief, anxiety or guilt.

■ Difficulty controlling anger, irritability and hostility.

■ Suspiciousness and mistrust of others; 'hypervigilance'.

■ Avoiding or withdrawing from other people.

■ Avoiding places or situations that remind you of the events.

■ Disturbed sleep – trouble sleeping or nightmares.

■ 'Flashbacks' in which you feel as if the disaster is happening all over again.

■ Overusing or abusing drugs or alcohol.

■ Impaired concentration or memory.

■ Multiple somatic (bodily) ailments, such as headaches, backaches, whole body aches, feelings of hotness or coldness in the body, faintness, heart palpitations, diarrhea, constipation, stomach pain or sexual difficulties.

■ Increased conflict with your spouse or friends or fellow workers or even strangers in the community.

It cannot be over-emphasized that these responses in the wake of traumatic events are perfectly *normal*. They are not a sign of mental illness or of weakness. It is the event you experienced that was abnormal, not your response. A very sizeable proportion of humanitarian workers develop such symptoms, either as a result of direct traumatization or as secondary traumatization. In especially horrendous situations, almost everyone develops some of these symptoms.

Normal though they are, these responses to both primary and secondary traumatization are more severe, more long lasting and more distressing than responses to the accumulation of day-in-day-out stress. If you do have lasting symptoms that continue to distress you or interfere with your ability to do your job, you should know that effective treatment is available. Ask your doctor or your supervisor or manager to help you find a qualified professional to assist you.

Secondary (vicarious) traumatization

You may also be adversely affected by your role as witness to the sufferings of others. You may be exposed to many heart-rending scenes. You are constantly exposed to the powerful emotions and harrowing tales of the survivors of horrific experiences. You may identify with them and share their emotions. After prolonged exposure to such experiences and tales, you may experience 'vicarious' or 'secondary' traumatization – i.e., emotional responses much like those of the primary survivors themselves.

Secondary traumatization is very common among humanitarian workers. For instance, more than 80 per cent of the rescue workers who had to deal with the bodies of victims of one air crash showed some post-traumatic symptoms and more than half showed moderately severe symptoms. Almost two years after the crash, a fifth of the rescue workers still had distressing symptoms. Another study of staff of humanitarian aid workers who had recently completed their assignments found that a third showed signs of stress severe enough to affect their work and 13 per cent apparently met the criteria for a diagnosis of post-traumatic stress disorder.

Barriers to recognizing your own distress

For many humanitarian workers, it is easier to recognize that other people are under stress than to see the effects it has on ourselves. To allow ourselves to be aware of our own vulnerability is very hard. Our professional identity as humanitarian workers depends on maintaining a sense of our own strength and resilience. Allowing ourselves to feel and express our deepest hidden feelings, our fears and angers and sense of inadequacy, can seem like a sign of weakness. It challenges our self respect or makes us feel like you are letting down others or letting down the people we are trying to help. We may feel guilty, because the stresses experienced by those we are there to help seem so much greater than our own. It is easier to see ourselves as helpers than to acknowledge that we, too, could use support. After a while, we may 'habituate' to stress – it seems like 'the way of the world' and there is nothing that can be done about it. Our impulse is to deny feelings, distract ourselves and 'get on with the job that has to be done'. Letting others know our feelings is harder still. It is shaming and it feels like it might expose us to ridicule.

But 'nature driven out through the door comes back through the window', wrote the French philosopher Charles Fourier. In the end, no matter how much we may want to suppress or disguise our stress reactions, they affect our work and our happiness. We may acknowledge them or they may appear in disguised form, such as unproductive hyperactivity, feelings of physical exhaustion, cynicism, 'black humor', lack of energy to accomplish tasks, psychosomatic disorders, sleep disturbances, difficulty concentrating or solving problems, or careless or reckless actions that endanger others and ourselves. It is important to remember that we are human beings and that having strong feelings as a result of extended periods of humanitarian work is part of being human.

Reduce the stresses of humanitarian work

If you are a humanitarian worker, there is no escaping stress. But remember: the effects of stress are cumulative. Every stressor you can eliminate or make less stressful lessens the overall burden of stress upon you. Lessening the burden of chronic stress reduces the likelihood of adverse reactions, including burnout.

How do you reduce your stress load?

1. 'Be prepared'
The same event or situation is more stressful if it is unexpected than if it is expected.

The closer your expectations are to the realities you will face, the greater your sense of predictability and control, the less your feelings of helplessness and uncertainty will be. The more prepared you are before taking up your assignment and the more prepared you are each day for the challenges you face that day, the more likely you will be able to deal effectively with the emotional challenges of humanitarian work. You need to know to what to expect, both practically and emotionally, in yourself and in the people you will be helping.

Learn as much as you can about the particular situation in which you will be working (see pp. 8–9). Before you ever get to the field, it is very helpful to talk to others who have had direct experience of the particular work you will be doing. What kind of experiences should you expect? When you get to your assignment, ask colleagues and staff of other agencies about what to expect. Get information that is as specific as possible. The better able you are to picture potential sources of stress, the better you will be at dealing with them if and when they occur. In addition to learning about the details of your work assignment, learn about the political and social and military context and about the local power structure – formal and informal, military and civilian.

If you come from a country or cultural environment different from that in which you will be working, learn as much as you can about the latter (see pp. 9–13). Learning about how people in that culture express emotions and about conventional rules of social behavior – for example, how people greet each other, assumptions about eye contact and physical distance, assumptions about responding to demands or saving face – is especially important.

Although it is helpful to learn as much as you can about what you will face even before you leave for your assignment, most learning about the stressors in particular situations will be done 'on the ground'. Do not worry excessively if you cannot get as much information as you would like before you leave, but stay especially open to learning during the first months of your assignment.

2. Identify sources of stress
Be pro-active in trying to eliminate those that can be eliminated and in trying to reduce the impact of those that cannot be eliminated altogether.

If you look back to the list of the stresses of humanitarian work (pp. 72–73), you will see that some of the sources of stress come from the situation in which humanitarian work is done, others from things the humanitarian agency does or does not do. It is a mistake to place the responsibility for reducing stress entirely on the individual aid worker. A large part of the responsibility is with the agency that employs you.

To reduce stress on staff, your organization should:

- Reduce bureaucracy and paperwork as much as possible.

- Provide adequate information about the overall humanitarian emergency in which you will be working.

- Provide adequate information about the specific tasks you will be asked to do and appropriate training to enable you to do them.

- Be clear as to work roles and organizational responsibilities.

- Provide adequate supplies for the work demanded.

- Develop work rules and schedules that permit you to follow through on task assignments.

- Consult with staff – local as well as expatriate – with regard to policies and programs.

- Facilitate communication between staff and their own families.

- Provide adequate facilities for rest, sleep, washing and eating.

- Provide adequate food, shelter and rest time for staff.

- Intervene in the environment to reduce noise, improve traffic flow and provide space to take a break.

- Have an adequate safety and security guidelines in place and make sure that all staff follow them.

- Promote a sense of camaraderie and mutual respect and support among staff.

- Intervene to 'defuse' conflicts among workers or between staff members and their supervisors.

- Have clear policies to prohibit sexual harassment and conflict or harassment based on ethnicity or national origin, with appropriate grievance procedures in place to enforce them.

- Provide recognition and appreciation for the sacrifices the staff members are making.

A detailed set of 'Guidelines for good practice by humanitarian agencies in managing staff stress' can be found in the Resources. Agencies that comply with these guidelines are doing their part to support staff. If your agency does not provide these supports, ask it to.

At a more individual level, be self-conscious about what you can do to lessen the stress you face. Try to identify your own weak points and vulnerabilities. If a certain kind of issue 'pushes your buttons', or if certain themes – for example, survivor guilt – recur over and over, recognize the effects and work on learning to manage the issue.

Set realistic goals for yourself. Know your own limits. Do not be afraid to say 'no'. Do not push yourself to carry on no matter what, for example, if you are sick. Ask yourself, 'Is this task necessary? Is it useful? Does it justify the risk or effort needed to do it?' Be prepared to dump inessential tasks, or delay doing them or delegate them. But with essential tasks, do not delay. Delay adds the stress of having something hanging over you to the stress of the task itself. 'Just do it.'

'Compartmentalize': Solve one problem and do one task at a time. Think positively about what you can do, even if it is only a small part of what needs to be done. Structure your use of time. Begin your day by reviewing yesterday's work, then plan today and tomorrow. Set priorities. Set realistic short-term and long-term goals and accept small goals. Try to accomplish something each day. Notice your own rhythms. Most of us have certain times of day when we are less efficient than others – for example, we are 'morning people' or 'afternoon people' or we have an 'energy dip' in mid-afternoon. Distribute your work accordingly, if possible.

Maintain your sense of curiosity about why problems develop, view your own personal problems with humility and take them as occasions for learning, and keep your sense of humor. Even when stresses seem overwhelming, teach yourself to think consciously about the positive things in your life.

Remember the 'Serenity Prayer': *'God grant me the serenity to accept the things I cannot change; courage to change the things I can; and wisdom to know the difference'.* You can solve some problems and you can ease others if you have the courage to ask for help, but there are some problems you cannot do anything about.

3. Undertake personal actions that increase your fitness for dealing with the stresses you will inevitably experience

The first step is to identify your own individual responses to stress and monitor yourself. What are your own physiological responses to stress – for example, headaches, tension in your shoulders, stomach upsets? What thoughts signal to you that you are under stress – for example, 'I can't', or 'I've had enough'? Do you engage in characteristic behaviors, such as talking too much or drinking or smoking more than usual? Do you get irritable and find yourself snapping at others? Do you engage in risky behaviors, such as driving too fast or engaging in unprotected sex? These are signs to rethink your goals and how you are going about meeting them. When you see your level of stress increasing, take action to reduce it. It can also be helpful to use a 'buddy system'. Agree with a friend or colleague to watch each other for signs of stress. Agree that you will tactfully point out to each other if you see the other becoming 'stressed out' and that you will suggest a course of action.

Next, identify the sources of stress you will face, as specifically as possible. Although some sources of stress are totally unpredictable, most of them are predictable, at least in general terms. Make a list: think ahead, on a daily and hourly basis. What challenges are you likely to face? How will you try to deal with them? Think though what your response would be – for example, at a roadblock or if local officials seek to interfere with your work. Rehearse your responses, either in your mind or with a friend.

Third, undertake actions that strengthen you in dealing with stressors.

■ *Try to ensure you have some private and/or personal space to retreat into* – to read, think, write, meditate, listen to music or just stare into space. Separate your office (work) space and your personal (living) space. As much as possible, make both your living accommodations and your office space personal and comfortable – a refuge. For example, mementos from home help to keep you centered.

■ *Build a social support system.* Spend time with colleagues, not only during working hours and not necessarily focused on work. Talk or e-mail or write to friends and colleagues who have had experiences similar to yours. Keep in touch with family and friends. Keep an eye out for colleagues – helping them helps you and you may need their watchful eye or support. Try to have varied social contacts; cultivate friendships beyond the circle of your immediate colleagues. Be aware, though, that in intense situation, strong personal relationships often develop. Such relationships can be important in coping, but be careful and consider the consequences for other relationships you may have at home and the effects on colleagues. Also be aware of local customs and taboos.

■ *Stay physically fit.* Get enough rest and enough sleep. Taking time away from your assignment to rest may seem like a frivolous use of your time, but it helps you work at maximum efficiency and do your job better and with fewer errors. Maintain proper nutrition. Limit junk food. Try to sit down and eat your meals at a more or less regular time, rather than eating while 'on the run'. Do not get into the habit of eating when you are emotionally upset. Get regular exercise and keep in shape. Exercise, walk, jog, dance, stretch, do yoga, work out, play volleyball. Stay healthy: do not delay pursuing any specific healthcare needs you have. If you get sick, seek appropriate care. Maintain any medication regimens you have previously been prescribed. Maintain your personal hygiene – for example, bathing, brushing your teeth, keeping your clothes clean.

■ *Avoid the temptation to use alcohol or drugs or risky sex to 'escape the pressures' of your work.* (Unless it is necessary for medical or cultural/religious reasons, there is no reason to abstain entirely). Drug and alcohol use and sex may seem to offer an immediate escape from distress, anxiety or depression, but if you find that these are the only ways you can survive the pain, anxiety, rage, fear or other distress created by your work, *ask for help.*

■ *Limit coffee to two cups a day.* Caffeine increases anxiety. Remember that tea, cola drinks and chocolate also have caffeine in them.

■ *Slow down and relax.* Take work breaks during the day. If at all possible, these should be taken away from your work site – for example, in a separate tent on the edge of the relief operation site, or in a room in the back of a shelter. Schedule time to relax at the end of the day, too. Take off at least one day a week and a few days every four to six weeks. Use your vacation time – people who brag that 'I haven't taken a vacation in two years' are setting themselves up for disaster. Take time for non-work activities, such as a hobby or keeping a journal. Develop leisure-time interests and give yourself time to enjoy them – board games, reading, bird watching, discussion groups, local culture and history, musical instruments, etc. Learn the local language. Keep a diary – it is a way of letting off steam and it helps you look at your daily experience with some perspective. Try deep breathing, stretching, muscle relaxation or meditation. 'Take time to smell the flowers'. It is hard for many humanitarian workers to take days off, much less vacations. They may feel that taking time off is a 'slap in the face' to the recipients of assistance, who cannot take a break from their experience. But remember – the many aspects of a humanitarian worker's life that *differentiate* you from recipients are there whether or not you take a few days off. Putting the burden of blame for the differences solely on your ability to take a vacation misses the point entirely.

■ *Be culturally open and show respect for the community you are working in.* Be flexible and patient and non-judgmental. 'Different' is not 'bad'. Try to learn at least a few words of the local language. Befriend local people. If you find yourself withdrawing or having a sense of superiority, however well you think you are hiding it, catch yourself. But also beware of over-identification with the local culture.

The suggestions above reflect approaches to preparing to deal with stress and to relieving stress that are based on the experience of Europeans and North Americans. Most of them will apply to those from other cultures just as well. But people from other cultures – and more than a few people from Europe or North America, as well – may find that other ways of dealing with stress are more effective. For example, you may find that taking time off to deal with family needs is a better way of reducing stress than 'taking a vacation' or that time with others or engaging in a familiar ritual relaxes you more than getting off by yourself. Do not read the suggestions above as a series of 'oughts'. Identify your own best ways of preparing for stress and pursue them.

4. Make your work team work

Your work team is your single greatest resource in times of crisis and your single greatest source of support when you are stressed out. Every member of the team bears responsibility for making the team 'work'.

Every team has at least minor conflicts. Try to manage minor conflicts before they become major conflicts. Handling a negative relationship with one or two other individuals on your team can be tricky. If you are on a short-term assignment, the best strategy may be to 'live and let live'. But if you are on a long-term assignment, you need to deal with it. Do not take the burden entirely upon yourself. Enlist managerial support, not to achieve a victory but to create a smoother way of dealing with each other.

People cannot read your mind. It is your responsibility to communicate your needs, wishes and ideas.

1 Tell others your needs and ask what they need.

2 Share information. Secrets are deadly in a group.

3 Check your own level of impatience with the different communication styles of others. Realize the communication styles of others are not used to purposely annoy you.

4 You have a right to your own opinions, to feel and express pain, to ask for change, to say 'no', to choose not to respond to a situation.

5 Be sure to be respectful of others' needs to express their own feelings and opinions, too.

Working with others always involves negotiation. A good starting point for successful negotiation is to recognize that building and maintaining trust and understanding and respect is as important as solving the problem. Focus on the problem or issue, not personalities. Avoid personal attacks.

Avoid undermining others. This is one of the greatest threats to maintaining a healthy work environment. Avoid language that suggests that you are the only one being fair and reasonable and that others are being unfair or unreasonable. Concentrate on finding solutions rather than determining blame. Do not try to solve all problems at once – proceed step by step. Try to identify common goals and interests before you focus on differences. Encourage people to be explicit about their differences in opinion. Generate a variety of options before making decisions and try to restate other's positions to be sure you understand them. Be ready to ask for clarification and to say 'I don't know' or 'I don't understand'. Let others know your own motives: helping them to understand why you are making a suggestion avoids guessing and suspicion. Summarize and restate agreements to be sure you all understand what you have concluded.

Two particularly problematic intra-staff issues are sexual harassment and harassment, teasing, hostility, conflict or discrimination related to ethnicity or national origin. Either one creates an intimidating, hostile or offensive environment and interferes with work. When they occur, it is a major source of stress for their targets. Do not ignore harassment or discrimination at work, whether directed at you or at one of your colleagues. There are several possible courses of action – see Chapter 2, pp. 47–49 for some suggestions on dealing with sexual harassment. The same principles apply equally well to other forms of harassment.

Another potentially problematic intra-staff issue arises from the differences in the experience of international staff and national (local) staff. National staff members face a variety of stressors that expatriates do not, often including concerns for the safety and well-being of their family and exposure to intra-community tensions. Local staff may also feel less job security, resentment that they are paid less or receive fewer benefits, resentment that they are not given the same level of training and protection by the agency, and resentment that they receive less information from and are not consulted by the agency. Their own personal and family history during the events that has given rise to the humanitarian mission may make them more vulnerable to revivals of their own traumatization when faced by the stories of those they seek to help.

The often unspoken tensions created by these differences have an adverse impact on both local and international staff. A disgruntled employee can interfere with effective team functioning, can create a source of danger to the team, and can impede the ability of the team to provide mutual support. There are no magical solutions that wipe away the differences in the experience of local and international staff, but pretending the differences do not exist may be as stressful for local staff as the differences themselves. Appreciative inquiry about local staff members' needs, needed resources and organizational and personal concerns and an attitude of humility, interest, mutual respect and transparency, together with a desire for consultation and true partnership is a good starting place for lessening these tensions.

Cope with the stresses of humanitarian work

No matter how well you prepare, stress is inevitable in humanitarian work. The better able you are to cope with it, the less distress you will experience and the less likely it is that you will suffer long term consequences, for example, burnout.

Coping with stress can take many forms. When it is possible to do something about the *cause* of your distress, do it. Taking action simultaneously reduces the external challenge and reduces your own subjective sense of distress. But for many of the predictable and not-so-predictable stresses of humanitarian work, there is little you can do to eliminate the stressor itself. In these circumstances, you have to undertake activities to protect yourself from the adverse effects of the stress. You can undertake an activity that diverts your thoughts away from what is disturbing you, or you can undertake activities that more directly reduce the unpleasant arousal that stress creates in you. You are allowed to do both.

Diversion/distraction
One simple approach to reducing stress is to do something that takes your attention away from the source of anxiety. Focus on a pleasant thought or image to drive the unpleasant thoughts and images and the impossibility of doing all that has to be done from your head, or engage in an activity that diverts your attention away from the source of anxiety. Play a game, go to a movie, read a book, go dancing, exercise, talk with a friend.

Arousal reduction
A second approach to reducing tension is to do something that directly reduces tension. The logic is that you cannot be both stressed out and relaxed at the same time, so if you do something positive to relax yourself, you are, at the same time, reducing your stress level.

For many people, talking about stressful experiences helps reduce the anxiety they create. Talk to a friend, a co-worker or a supervisor about your experiences and your needs. What is stressing you out? What are you thinking about it? What are you feeling? What information do you need? What support do you need? Talking helps give you perspective. It gives you a feeling of support. It may help you think of alternative action plans that you had not thought of before. It may help you get rid of thoughts that your failure to change the situation is due to a personal failing. And it just feels good to 'ventilate' – to get our feelings out in a non-judgmental situation. Your agency may offer a more structured way of talking about stressful experiences. These may be called 'defusing' or 'debriefing' procedures. 'Defusing' is a group intervention carried out within a few hours of any unusual interpersonal incident – for example, a conflict between aid workers or between workers and victims – or other unusual stressful incident – for example, an accident injuring a worker. 'Debriefing' is a more extended group intervention. It may be carried out after a particularly traumatic event or on a regularly scheduled basis, for example, once a month. You should certainly be offered a debriefing session before you return home to your 'regular' life or move on to another assignment (but see the footnote on p. 88). Many people find 'brief relaxation' techniques helpful. These are very brief exercises meant to be done 'on the run'. Practice any of them as often as you like to stop the build up of stress and to help you re-center yourself and refocus your thoughts. They are especially useful if you are getting angry. Sample scripts for several brief relaxation exercises can be found in the Resources.

Most people also find more extended 'relaxation exercises' helpful. These exercises take five to 10 minutes to do. Even in a crisis situation, doing one of these exercises is often an effective use of time. After doing the exercise you will be better able to concentrate and to make decisions more efficiently and with better judgment. It is also helpful to do these exercises on a *routine* daily basis – for example, once in the morning, once in the afternoon or early evening. Doing so reduces your overall stress level, reduces the likelihood of burnout and enables you to cope better with acute stressors.

There are several major types of extended relaxation exercise – for example, visualization, breathing and muscle relaxation, meditation. It does not matter which you use. Choose the type that you feel comfortable with.

In a visualization exercise, you think about a situation in which you feel safe and relaxed – for example, walking in the woods or along the beach or sitting with your family on your front porch. You imagine all the parts of this scene in a very detailed way – the colors, shapes, sounds, textures, smells, temperature and feel. *It is critically important that you use a scene that is safe and relaxing to you.* If, for instance, you find walking in the woods frightening, do not use a visualization scene involving walking in the woods. Instead, write your own comparable script using the situation that you find safe and relaxing.

In a breathing and muscle relaxation exercise, you breathe in a controlled way, while attending closely to your breathing. This can be combined with a muscle relaxation exercise: You first contract a group of muscles – for example, the muscles of your right arm – for 10 seconds or so and then relax them while concentrating on the feelings of relaxation. You continue to do this with different groups of muscles until your entire body is relaxed.

In a meditation exercise, you pick a word or phrase or meaningless sound – for example, the number 'one' or the phrase 'relax' or the sound 'ommmm'. Sit in a relaxed position and focus on your breathing. Each time you exhale, say the word or phrase or sound you have chosen to yourself, concentrating on it. You may find that your mind drifts into other thoughts. That is fine – simply notice that you have drifted away and return to the meditation phrase. Continue for 10 to 15 minutes.

Whatever kind of relaxation exercise you choose, start with a script. Sample scripts can be found in Resources. You can use these scripts as is or adapt them. Ask someone to read the script to you, in a slow calm voice, while you do the exercise. Or read your script into a tape recorder and carry out the exercise while listening to your own tape. After a while, you will not need the script. You can also buy commercial relaxation tapes at many book stores or over the internet or download audio files of relaxation exercises directly from the internet (see Resources for sources).

Burnout

The best prevention for burnout is to follow the suggestions for reducing your stress load and improving your coping discussed above. If, despite your best efforts, you do begin see signs of burnout in yourself (see above, pp. 73–75), taking some time for rest and relaxation and a change of routine may provide relief. It may be helpful to seek out a different kind of assignment in which you use your skills but also develop new ones. For instance, working in an office-based job with your agency for a period of time may get you ready to face the field again.

Critical incident (traumatic incident) intervention

Most of what we have said so far is about dealing with ordinary, although possibly pretty intense, stress. Sometimes the incidents that cause stress are far from ordinary. They involve direct threats to your life or physical well-being or witnessing threats to the life or well-being of someone else. In such moments, we feel terror, horror, rage, intense powerlessness and other intense emotions. Even though you survive the incident, you are no longer quite the same. You may continue to feel like a 'survivor' for days or weeks after the event and you may be troubled with lasting painful or disruptive symptoms. (See above, pp. 74–77, for more on traumatic stress.) Most of these symptoms are temporary and will resolve on their own, although it may take a few weeks or even months, and most people can still carry on in their regular job, with some support and encouragement.

After experiencing such an event, the best way of preventing serious long term consequences is immediate action.

- Get away from the immediate scene of the event; allow yourself some brief rest and respite and physical replenishment – for example, sleep, food. In the immediate wake of the event, you are probably in no shape, emotionally, cognitively and physically to process what has happened to you. Try to calm yourself. You may want to use some of the relaxation techniques described above.

- Understand that significant and possibly distressing psychological reactions are *normal* after this kind of situation. They are not a sign of weakness *on your part* or evidence of something seriously wrong with you. It is the event that was abnormal, not you.

- Talk about what happened. After a critical incident, your agency should offer immediate – within a few days – support, from a counselor who has been trained in providing such support. The support program may be called 'psychological first aid' or 'crisis intervention' or 'defusing' or 'stress debriefing'. Regardless of the name, it is essentially a way of checking in on how you are doing and getting you to talk about your experiences on an individual basis or with a group. You will be asked to talk about what happened, what you are thinking and feeling now, and what kind of support you need or want. Request that your agency provide such a debriefing if you are not offered one.[1]

  If such a formal process is not offered and is not available, try to find someone who has been through a similar experience and who is willing to *listen* empathically to you.

  If someone else on your team has experienced a traumatic event, encourage them to talk about their thoughts. Do not be insistent if they do not want to talk, but you might go back a few hours or a day later and try again. Allow them as much time as they need to talk. Be non-judgmental. And listen, listen, listen with undivided attention. Strongly encourage their participation in any structured program – for example, 'debriefing' – offered by your agency. If they remain seriously distressed after a few days, encourage them to seek professional assistance and help them find it.

- Do not take your terrible experience as an excuse to 'go home'. It may be tempting, but in most cases you are better off dealing with the feelings in the overall environment where they occurred – but not at the actual scene of the events. Plan to return to work promptly. Remember: you still have responsibilities to your team and, in turn, your team is your best source of social support.

---

[1] There is a lot of controversy among mental health professionals – and not a whole lot of empirical data – as to the best way of preventing long-term adverse consequences from traumatic events. What can be said with some certainty is this: (1) If you feel that a debriefing procedure suggested by your agency is making you feel worse or 'out of control', stop it. (2) 'One-shot' or 'one-off' interventions are less effective than interventions that provide repeated opportunities to talk about your experiences and to get support. If you are only offered a single crisis intervention session, ask for a follow up session a few days or a few weeks later. (3) New forms of intervention are being developed. Do not be surprised if your agency proposes a somewhat different model of immediate intervention.

- If you find that the weeks go by and you are continuing to suffer from a severe stress reaction, do not suffer in silence, do not allow yourself to think that your failure to heal is your fault, and do not imagine that others will think badly of you. *Seek professional help.* Your doctor or your supervisor or manager should be able to help you find an appropriately trained professional.

Spiritual resources for humanitarian workers

by James Guy and Amber Elizabeth Gray

For many humanitarian workers, spiritual resources provide a powerful tool for coping with the stresses of humanitarian work. This is a complicated matter, however: catastrophic events can severely test a person's spiritual beliefs as well. A catastrophic event can destroy the sense of safety, security and stability that is fundamental for a sense of personal well-being. A natural disaster such as an earthquake or famine reminds us of how vulnerable we are to forces beyond our control. A human-made disaster, such as warfare or genocide, reveals the shocking potential for cruelty inherent in each of us. In both cases, survivors are left to sort out their basic feelings and beliefs as a consequence of the trauma and suffering associated with catastrophic occurrences. For each person, the underlying sense of trust and connection changes following a disaster. Their world views and belief systems are altered forever. This often leads to a shift in religious beliefs or practices, as survivors attempt to incorporate the apparent silence or impotence of God or Spirit in the face of the tragic events. These shifts can increase or, conversely, diminish a survivor's sense of faith, at least initially.

As survivors try to 'make sense out of it all' and go on with their lives, they confront spiritual and existential questions: Why did this happen? What is the meaning of this event? What does this event reveal about human nature? What does it suggest about God? How can God permit evil in the world? What will the future bring? How is hope possible? These are not idle questions. A sense of meaning and purpose can bring comfort, perspective, hope and resolution and may be the most important aspect of emotional recovery following a disaster. This has led a number of experts in the field of traumatic stress to conclude that personal spirituality is a determining variable in the experience of traumatic stress and later recovery. Conversely, a lack of meaning and purpose can lead to despair, hopelessness, and a profound sense of aloneness.

Like the direct survivors of catastrophes, humanitarian workers also struggle with issues related to transcendence, meaning and purpose. Regardless of the exact nature of your assignment, as a humanitarian worker you will directly and repeatedly be confronted with the senseless suffering of victims and the apparent meaninglessness of catastrophic events. You will see firsthand, on a large scale, the consequences of both natural and human-made disasters. The capricious forces of nature and the cruel actions of human beings directly oppose the deep sense of compassion and idealism that drives you to help others.

The Humanitarian Companion

To go on with your work with sufficient vitality and commitment, you must find acceptable answers to the same questions of meaning and purpose that confront the survivors you serve. Or, perhaps you must learn to live with the absence of meaningful answers. Regardless, it is useful to attend to spiritual issues as part of a comprehensive plan for ongoing self-care.

Spirituality is a core component of human nature. It includes a sense of meaning and purpose, hope and faith. It is a central basis and motivation for morality, personal growth and service to others. For some, the experience of spirituality involves a personal relationship with a deity, such as would be found in organized religion. For others, it may be best described as a sense of transcendence or relationship with the encompassing universe or origin of existence. For still others, the core of spiritual belief is their relationship with nature or their faith in the ability of human beings to survive and even prevail in the face of horrors.

Whether due to an explicit belief in God or a more diffuse sense of awareness of the non-physical or a belief in human solidarity, most individuals believe that to be fully human involves more than the physical dimension of existence. This sense of personal spirituality is paradoxically both a private, individual matter and a near universal human experience. Thus, it is possible for many relief organizations to incorporate spirituality in their human resources programs regardless of the individual religious beliefs of their staff or the orientation of the organization itself. For those with more highly structured religious practices and beliefs, a natural or human-made disaster often necessitates a complete reconsideration of the premises and conclusions upon which their religious experience is based. Traumatic stress may disrupt long-held beliefs about the nature of God and humankind. Left unattended, the despair normally associated with trauma may be exacerbated and complicated by a loss of faith.

For those with a more general sense of spirituality unrelated to personal religious practice, traumatic stress following a catastrophic event can be a catalyst for either a deeper evolving spiritual awareness or a growing cynicism, callousness or despair. No one path is right for all, but the following suggestions are some simple ways to incorporate personal spirituality into a comprehensive self-care plan.

- Seek out easily accessible pastoral counseling, spiritual direction and local congregational support.

- Create a ritual that has meaning for you, to be practiced individually and/or collectively. Designate a consistent time each day to honor your spiritual practice. This might be personal prayer or meditation or a group spiritual practice, such as chanting, singing, prayer, dance and drumming.

- For many people, structured forms of meditation, yoga, tai chi or progressive relaxation can facilitate a spiritual connection. Set aside a specific room or space that is reserved for such spiritual practice, meditation and reflection. Engage in the activity every day.

- The arts are considered to be sacred, spiritual practices in many cultures. In the absence of more 'conventional' western or organized forms of worship, you may find it helpful to devote off-duty time to exploring spirituality through mediums such as music, painting, theater, dance and poetry.

- Create opportunities for team members to teach one another about their differing world views, experiences of personal spirituality, religious traditions and spiritual practices.

- Create a non-hierarchical structure for worship or community prayer/gathering on-site, based on collective input and needs from all who might participate. The Quaker meeting model can be a useful template. But note that in groups who come from many differing religious traditions, common prayer may be impossible. A common structure enabling people to come together but then to split into smaller groups or sit on their own for prayer may work better than an attempt to establish a completely common ritual.

When working alongside colleagues from other countries, it is important to consider other world views when discussing the meaning of disaster and trauma. For example, in many cultures that are less individually oriented than those of Western Europe and North America, community and collective rituals may be considered essential for a healthy developmental progression through life. They are regarded as instrumental in navigating challenging, difficult life passages such as traumatic events.

By encouraging staff to devote time to nurturing their personal spirituality, leaders of humanitarian organizations demonstrate their awareness of the value of such pursuits for most individuals. This can be done respectfully and 'inclusively', in a non-coercive way, adding an important component to comprehensive wellness and self-care programs.

CHAPTER 5

Working with survivors of traumatic experiences

The 'culture of traumatization'

Gathering information without re-traumatizing
    Some general principles of interviewing
    Some specific techniques for interviewing trauma survivors

Working with survivors of humanitarian emergencies
    Some general principles for humanitarian work

Some cross-cultural issues

Humanitarian workers work with people who have survived terrible experiences – natural disasters, famines, accidents with mass casualties, war, civil war and ethnic cleansing, political oppression, terrorist attacks, individual rapes and other assaults, being uprooted from their homes and forced to flee.

The physical consequences of these catastrophes are usually obvious. Schools, hospitals and power stations are destroyed, and workplaces, livestock and other means of making a living are wrecked. The direct effect on the bodies of the victims is equally evident. People are killed or severely injured. The immediate emotional effects – shock, numbness, anger – are also clear.

As the weeks and months go by, the physical effects of the survivors' experiences may fade. Houses are rebuilt, roads repaired, communications systems restored. For most survivors, the bodily wounds, too, heal. But the emotional wounds – the wounds to the heart, the wounds to the soul – may last.

Except for psychosocial workers, most aid worker's assignments are not explicitly focused on helping survivors of catastrophes heal emotionally. However, the policies and programs of humanitarian agencies and the ways in which you as an individual humanitarian worker carry out your tasks may make a major contribution to helping the survivors heal or, at least, to helping the survivors deal better with the emotional wounds they have suffered. Alternately, despite your best intentions, your actions may worsen the situation and interfere with the survivors' ability to heal.

For all kinds of humanitarian workers, the emotional state of the survivors of a disaster has an enormous effect on their ability to cooperate with relief, recovery and reconstruction efforts. Just as understanding people's culture enables you to be more effective in your work, understanding what could, metaphorically, be called the 'culture of traumatization' contributes to your effectiveness as a humanitarian worker. As any humanitarian worker knows – or learns quickly, as soon as they start working in the field – survivors of terrible experiences are not necessarily easy to work with. In some cases, an individual may have been 'difficult' long before the catastrophic events occurred. But it is not uncommon for individuals who have had terrible experiences to show signs of irritability, suspiciousness, apathy or uncooperativeness. Understanding these reactions helps you to 'not take it personally' and to work more effectively.

In this chapter we will look, in some detail, at the emotional states the people humanitarian workers work with are likely to experience. Then we will look at what happens when humanitarian workers interview or otherwise seek to gather information from the survivors of a disaster. Finally, we will examine how humanitarian workers can structure their day-to-day work with the survivors to enhance the latter's ability to heal and, at the same time, to enhance their own effectiveness.

The 'culture of traumatization'[1]

Survivors of prolonged and severe traumatic experience may show very complex and persistent mixes of psychological symptoms. For some, chronic grief, depression, anxiety or guilt dominates. For others, difficulties controlling anger, suspiciousness, irritability and hostility prevail. Yet others mistrust or avoid or

---

[1] The phrase 'culture of traumatization' needs comment. I do not mean to imply that the problems faced by survivors of terrible events are solely or even primarily due to the psychological effects of more-or-less discrete traumatic events in their recent past. Such a perspective would obscure the fact that survivors of traumatic events are usually also survivors of long experience with poverty, powerlessness and oppression, stretching back many generations. Their troubles did not begin with the recent 'traumatic' events that may have occasioned the humanitarian intervention. It would also obscure the fact that they continue to face very concrete 'post-trauma' ongoing problems, such as poverty, illness or poor health (including HIV/AIDS), lack of the means to make a living, grief over losses of family, friends and community, and realistic fears of further threats to their physical safety. Their own inability and the inability of the humanitarian community to solve these problems are the primary determinants of their mental state.

At the same time, to entirely reject the notion of a 'culture of traumatization' – even with the emendations noted above – would ignore the fact that traumatic experiences of all kinds, long past and recent, are internalized and can affect or become part of an individual's or a community's characteristic way of functioning. (It is all but impossible to separate out which emotional phenomena are the results of recent traumatic events and which are long standing). Failure to recognize this can lead to a belief that 'all' survivors need is changes in their current situation – i.e., food, shelter, and other resources, the offering of some degree of power, the pursuit of justice against perpetrators of atrocities – and healing, reconciliation, peace, prosperity and economic growth will automatically occur. The apathy, dependency, suspiciousness and irritability of some survivors and the ways interpersonal conflict and lack of community cohesion may interfere with effective humanitarian work become incomprehensible.

withdraw from other people. For many, sleep is disturbed by nightmares, the waking hours by flashbacks in which they feel as if the disaster is happening all over again. Amnesia and trance states are not uncommon. Some begin to abuse drugs or alcohol. Preoccupation with revenge or unrealistic attributions of total power to perpetrators of atrocities, or, paradoxically, gratitude toward the perpetrator may appear.

Often the most common complaints heard are somatic (bodily) rather than 'emotional'. Survivors complain of symptoms such as headaches, backaches, whole body aches, feelings of hotness or coldness in the body, faintness, heart palpitations, diarrhea, constipation, stomach pain or sexual difficulties. They may repeatedly seek help from a doctor or nurse. At the same time, they may not make complaints about their emotional state.

Another very common observation in the wake of horrendous events is increased marital conflict or community conflict. For instance, a wife may report increased conflict with her husband or being beaten by him, or a man or woman may complain that their spouse has acted violently towards their children. In the community, schoolyard disputes or marketplace quarrels may quickly escalate into fist fights or knife fights and there may be an increase in general violence and crime in the community. Because there is no open expression of distress related to the traumatic events, it is easy to misunderstand these behaviors as purely individual or familial, rather than as a disguised emotional effect of the trauma.

Beyond their effects on individuals, mass disasters affect families, communities and entire cultures. These events are characterized by the more-or-less simultaneous displacement of hundreds of thousands or even millions of people; the destruction of families, entire villages and traditional ways of life; the unraveling of pre-existing social structures, social roles, social arrangements and rituals; the terrorization and 'silencing' of victims and onlookers; the massive disruption of trusting connections with others; and other massive upheavals in human relationships and activities and in culture itself.

Traumatic events do not affect everyone in the same way. At an individual level, some may experience a disaster with few or no psychological consequences, while others will go through the same disaster and be emotionally devastated. Certain categories of people are especially vulnerable, however.

Women are especially vulnerable to violence. In war or ethnic cleansing situations, they may be specifically targeted for mass or repeated rape. Women also face a heightened risk of violence in the aftermath of disasters of all kinds. As family stress mounts, women may become more exposed to physical or emotional abuse from their spouse. Women may also be exposed to rape and other forms of violence while fleeing armed conflict or while in a shelter or refugee camp. In almost every society, victims of rape are stigmatized and, in some cases, they are severely punished. The consequences of revealing a rape may be as traumatic as the event itself. The victim may 'escape' into illness or become socially isolated. Rape also has direct consequences, possibly including physical injury, acquisition of sexually transmitted disease – including HIV/AIDS, pregnancy, or loss of virginity – in settings in which this may have profound cultural meaning. Women may have great difficulty talking about such assaults. Shame, fear and anger may prevent women from revealing these events. The woman may deny the occurrence of these events – those with herself as victim and those with another family member, such as a daughter, as victim – to protect herself or others. She may fail to seek medical assistance.

In many humanitarian aid situations – for example, shelters and refugee camps – women often get less assistance. The husband, as 'head' of the household, often becomes the conduit for assistance to the family, which may or may not be equitably shared within the family. In some instances of food shortage, women have been given the lowest priority for getting a portion of what food is available. Discrimination with respect to food and medical attention in shelters and refugee camps has also been a problem in some instances. Healthcare facilities in shelters and refugee camps often do not attend to women's needs with regard to reproductive health. Providing for relief of other sources of strain on women, such as their responsibilities for childcare, often get a low priority.

In the aftermath of humanitarian emergencies, women who have been widowed by the traumatic events may find it harder to remarry than men. Lacking skills that are saleable in the paid job market, they may be left destitute. Alternately, husbands may leave the stricken community, seeking paid work elsewhere, leaving their wives more dependent on outside assistance and more isolated. Humanitarian emergencies, it should be emphasized, can create opportunities for women, as well. Women may have better social networks and hence, more social support than men. They may emerge as the leaders of grass-roots level organizations. They may be able to use humanitarian aid to develop skills and acquire tools and take on non-traditional roles. These changes are not without risk, however, since they may lead to intrafamily conflict.

The needs of women in humanitarian emergencies have to be understood in the context of their roles, experience and status in the pre-emergency society. At the same time, it should be stressed that not all women have the same needs. Differences in ethnicity, age, social class, marital status, as well as particular differences in personality or history of past trauma affect their needs. Elderly or disabled women may carry a double burden of vulnerability.

Most *children* respond sensibly and appropriately to disaster, especially if they experience the protection, support, and stability of their parents and other trusted adults. However, like adults, they may respond to disaster with a wide range of symptoms. Their responses are generally similar to those of adults, although they may appear in more direct, less disguised form. For example, they may engage in repetitive play in which the child re-enacts part of the disaster that has befallen them. Clinginess, social withdrawal, regressive behaviors such as bed wetting, sleep disturbances, irritability and aggressive behavior may appear.

One barrier to recognizing children's responses to disaster is the tendency of parents to misinterpret their children's reactions. To parents who are already under stress, a child's withdrawal, regression or misconduct may be understood as willful. Or, parents may not wish to be reminded of their own trauma or, seeking some small evidences that their life is again back in control, may have a need to see everything as 'all right'. In any of these cases, they may ignore or deny evidence of their children's distress.

Children who are orphaned or otherwise separated from their parents or other familiar caregivers are especially vulnerable. Unaccompanied children are vulnerable to neglect, exploitation and abuse. 'Protecting' children by sending them away 'for their own safety' adds the trauma of separation to the initial trauma. Those who have been forced to become 'child soldiers' may have experienced especially severe and repeated traumatization.

Depression and other forms of distress among the *elderly* are readily overlooked, in part because they may not take on exactly the same symptom pattern as among younger people, in part because the symptoms may be misunderstood as merely signs of age. For instance, disorientation, confusion, memory loss and distractibility may be signs of depression in the elderly. The elderly may also be especially vulnerable to being victimized. In the context of increased stress on the entire family, meeting their needs may take on a lowered priority.

One particular issue that may arise among the elderly is the feeling that they have lost their entire life – children, home, memorabilia – and that, due to their age, there is not enough time left in their life to rebuild and recreate. The elderly are also more likely to be physically disabled.

The *physically disabled*, the *mentally ill*, and the *mentally handicapped* are distinct groups with distinct needs and should not be lumped together. However, all three groups are at especially high risk in disasters and other humanitarian emergencies. For those in each group, the normal patterns of care or assistance that they receive and their own normal adaptations to produce acceptable levels of functioning are disrupted. For instance, supplies of medication, assistive devices such as wheelchairs, familiar caretakers and previously effective programs of treatment may become unavailable. This has both direct effects and increases anxiety and stress. Those who were mentally ill or developmentally delayed may also have fewer or less-adaptable coping resources available and less ability to mobilize help for themselves. The ongoing problems of the disabled may seem to the other survivors of the disaster to be of only minor importance in comparison to their own acute and unaccustomed suffering. Their disabilities may even seem like an obstacle to dealing with the disaster itself.

The disabled are especially vulnerable to marginalization, isolation and to 'secondary victimization'. They are at greater risk of post-disaster malnutrition, infectious disease – for example, in a shelter situation – and of the effects of lack of adequate healthcare.

Refugees and *internally displaced persons*, regardless of age or gender, have, typically, experienced personal terror or witnessed the physical abuse or death of loved ones. They have suffered the destruction of their homes and communities, the loss of their traditional livelihoods and the loss of material possessions. They may have been forcibly detained or spent periods in concentration camps and may, prior to arrival in the refugee camp, have been tortured, raped or otherwise physically abused. Their personal status, belief in themselves, trust in others and hopes for the future have been shattered. They feel vulnerable and mistrustful. They have become dependent on others for the physical necessities of life. In refugee camps, they may experience poor housing, disruption of personal networks, lack of medical care, interruption of their children's schooling, uncertainty regarding their rights and legal status and future. The refugee camp itself is likely to be a source of ongoing stress, with overcrowding, lack of privacy, poor sanitation, long periods of inactivity, noise, disrupted sleep and dangers of assault or rape. Those in camps for internally displaced persons and refugee camps on the borders of conflict zones may continue to live in conditions of extreme danger.

For both men and women, being a 'refugee' may prolong the trauma of whatever events threw them into refugee status and may interfere with natural processes of self-healing. They remain in a highly stressful, even repeatedly traumatic situation, and may have little prospect of escaping it. Just as with other forms of trauma, responses may vary from person to person. A central theme that may emerge is *mistrust*. The experience of many refugees has been that their trust has been repeatedly and violently violated. They have been exposed to death, danger and fear, often at the hands of neighbors or government officials. Initially, the refugee camp may seem like a haven, but after several weeks, with no permanent refuge in sight, the refugee's hopes seem once again to have been betrayed. In this context, feelings of anger, betrayal, skepticism and hostility are both common and normal. Refugees may express or enact distrust of camp officials, aid givers, mental health workers and relatives back home. Scapegoating, ostracizing others in the refugee camp or victimization of individuals or ethnic minorities may also occur. Apparently 'irrational' fears for personal safety may dominate behavior. For instance, a visit to a medical facility may trigger memories of torture experiences.

Horrendous experiences can also sometimes bring out the best in people and elicit strengths they have not shown previously. Many survivors feel an intense desire to help out in the recovery process. They may be willing to devote enormous energy to problem solving, on their own behalf and that of others. They search for meaningful acts and for new sources of meaning in their lives. New goals and values and priorities may appear.

Many survivors learn from their experience that they can handle a crisis effectively. They discover their own strengths. Some survivors may idealize those who helped rescue them and may aspire to be like them. They may feel an increased sense of connection to others and an increased appreciation of what has survived the disaster. These new behaviors, feelings and beliefs are especially common in the first weeks or months after a disaster, but in some individuals they may be long lasting. In part, at least, they may represent an effort to regain a sense of control, a sense of mastery. In any case, they represent an opportunity for those aiding survivors. Identifying those individuals whose responses are positive, and eliciting the positive element in the responses of all survivors, can play an important role in supporting humanitarian relief efforts. Note that the distinction between individuals who are 'traumatized' or who appear helpless and those who exhibit strength is not an absolute one. Some individuals may show both patterns, at different times or in different situations. The first weeks and months after a disaster, whether experienced in the survivor's own home or in a refugee camp or internally displaced persons camp, may constitute a 'honeymoon' period, in which the survivors are grateful for rescue and full of hope. As the weeks go by, however, reality sets in. Hope turns to disappointment, appreciation turns to anger, cooperation and enthusiasm turn into apathy and despair. This shift in the attitudes of those we seek to help may take the unprepared humanitarian worker by surprise.

Gathering information without re-traumatizing

Humanitarian workers and others working with the survivors of disasters – for example, community development workers, journalists – often seek to question the survivors of the disaster in order to gather information about what happened to them or what their needs are. To the aid worker, this is an entirely legitimate enterprise, one that is essential if they are to help those directly impacted by the disaster. But the process may look very different from the perspective of the person being questioned.

A barrage of questions from emergency and rescue workers, relatives and friends, humanitarian workers, healthcare workers, journalists, and/or human rights workers may be experienced by the person being questioned as intrusive, inappropriate, shaming or blaming. The person being interviewed may feel that answering questions opens them up to possible retaliation, stigmatization or ostracism. They may experience the questions as showing a lack of empathy, understanding, compassion or concern on the part of the interviewer, as cold, callous and uncaring. Questions or other aspects of interview process may trigger traumatic memories in the person being interviewed. These, in turn, can trigger intense fear, anxiety and other negative emotional reactions, which may prolong and intensify emotional traumatization.

An interview can be a source of misunderstanding between the persons being interviewed and the interviewer. The interviewer intends to gather information. The persons being interviewed may understand the purpose of the interview very differently. They may think that it is directly connected with their getting some concrete material aid – for example, help with housing or resettlement, job training or information about relatives – and may be disappointed when that goal is not met. They may feel that information is being gathered that could be used against them – for example, by the police – and may be suspicious of the interviewer's intentions. Conversely, the interviewer may feel he or she is being manipulated or 'used' by the person they are interviewing.

Humanitarian workers, almost by definition, have more power than those they interview. This includes immediate power (for example, control over material aid or information or access to justice) and a more tacit, implied power: humanitarian workers often come from a wealthy, powerful country (sometimes a country which, not so many years ago, held the recipient's country as a colony). They have education, income and access to those with power. And unlike the person being interviewed, they can escape the humanitarian emergency situation entirely, any time they want to. This power imbalance, especially in the context of the historical sense of powerless of many recipients of humanitarian assistance, permeates any interview. Interviewees may feel silenced or may be deferential or, conversely, may over-compensate for their powerlessness. They may seek to provide the answers they think the interviewee wants, or may seek to gain a sense of control over the situation by denying the interviewer the information the latter seeks, either openly or passively.

Some general principles of interviewing

To minimize the likelihood that dynamics like these will distort the interview, elicit inaccurate information, or harm the persons being interviewed, the following guidelines may be helpful.

- Start out by being self-aware about the interview and the interview process. Why are you interviewing this person at all? What is the purpose of the interview? What does the person being interviewed have to gain from being interviewed? What can you give the person being interviewed in return? (Information? Concrete help? An opportunity to talk? A sense that someone cares? Acknowledgement of suffering?). Be aware of your own prejudices, expectations, attitudes, experiences. You may feel uncomfortable about hearing certain things. As a result, your face or voice may, unknowingly, have the effect of discouraging the interviewee from talking about them. You may find that certain words, behaviors or emotional expressions 'trigger' irrationally intense reactions in you. These are perfectly normal reactions, but they may color your questions, reactions or understanding of what the interviewee means. Be aware of the asymmetry in your relationship: To you, the person you are interviewing may be one of dozens and the interview is just part of your job; to the person you are interviewing, talking to you is an unusual experience and may seem like a life and death matter.

- Before initiating an interview, learn the local cultural assumptions about how a stranger enters into a community. Are unannounced visits considered acceptable? Are you expected to approach an individual by going through village elders? Are you expected to approach a family member through the husband/father? What are the local beliefs about discussing personal problems, including mental health problems, with outsiders? What are the local idioms and metaphors people use to describe problems?

- An interview does not have to be cold, 'matter of fact', 'objective' in tone. Be empathic. Respond, reflect back the content and feelings expressed by the interviewee, attend, listen, observe, re-state.

■ Listen actively. Do not just listen to the words the person being interviewed says. Observe their body language and tone of voice. Try to understand what they are trying to convey and what it means to them. Open ended questions, for example, 'How did you feel when . . .?' are usually more useful than questions that can be answered 'yes' or 'no', for example, 'Did you feel sad when . . .?'. A 'yes' or 'no' answer may represent nothing more than an effort to be agreeable or may indicate that the person you are interviewing simply did not understand you.

■ Do not assume you understand what the person being interviewed is trying to say too quickly and do not anticipate what they will say or mean. Listen to what they actually say/mean. Ask questions to clarify what the interviewee is saying, such as 'In what way did you . . .?' 'What leads you to think that . . .?' 'Do you mean . . .?' 'Are you saying that . . .?' 'Then what happened?'. Reflect back – put into your own words – your understanding of what they are saying or feeling.

■ Be careful that your questions are not accusatory or suspicious or sarcastic in content or tone. Remember that irritability and suspiciousness and avoidance of painful topics are common *symptoms* in people who have had traumatic experiences. Monitor your own tone of voice, body language, mannerisms and behaviors throughout the interview. Avoid conveying boredom, irritation, impatience, anger, disgust, judgments. Avoid rudeness. Respond to the interviewee patiently, calmly, slowly, gently. Try to convey kindness and compassion, even when you are frustrated by difficulties in obtaining information or understanding the person you are interviewing.

■ Keep the interview focused gently, in accord with its purpose – is there specific information you need to elicit? Use questions or statements of clarification to re-focus interview, for example, ask the person being interviewed to elaborate on a particular point. Avoid 'why?' questions. Do not ask interviewee to justify his or her own behavior or feelings. Be non-judgmental: your aim is to gain information and understanding, not to pass judgments.

■ If you are interviewing a person who does not come from your own cultural group, be aware of the language and modes of expression of thoughts and feelings of the interviewee's culture. For example, how do you ask questions? Are direct questions shaming? Is there a cultural inhibition on disagreeing? Be aware of conventional expectations regarding personal space, eye contact, touching, modes of greeting and beginning a 'serious' conversation in the interviewee's culture.

■ Be aware of issues regarding use of interpreters. Training and guiding interpreters is important.
  – Answering questions in the presence of a person from the interviewee's own community may create issues of confidentiality. Even if the interpreter is not from the interviewee's immediate community, the interviewee may feel a sense of shame over revealing intimate history to a person of their own

culture. Be especially wary of using a family member to interpret, which may violate the family's sense of appropriate roles or boundaries.

– The interpreter may censor what the interviewee is saying, either to protect what they perceive as the interviewee's interests or to protect the 'interests' of the culture to which both interviewee and interpreter belong. Interpreters may tend to report what they *perceive* to be the meaning of the interviewee's statements rather than what the interviewee actually said, or may start to see themselves as experts who know what the interviewee should be answering.

– Even if none of these factors affect the interview process, linguistic issues having to do with the precise denotations and connotations of words may intrude. The interpreter's own trauma-related experiences and other responses to questions may affect the interview process. The specific relationship between interviewee and interpreter may also affect the process.

■ The gender and/or ethnicity of the interviewer may trigger or otherwise interact with the interviewee's experience. Decisions on who should interview whom should take this into account. For example, under almost all circumstance, female rape victims should be interviewed by a woman.

Some specific techniques for interviewing trauma survivors

Start out by greeting and welcoming the person you are interviewing, using the pattern appropriate to the particular culture. For instance, it may be considered rude to jump into questions designed to elicit factual information when you have not first exchanged a proper greeting, inquired about a person's health, inquired about their family, etc.

Introduce yourself. Explain why you are going to be asking them questions – the purpose of the interview. Tell the person you are interviewing exactly what is going to happen in the interview – for example, the kinds of questions you will be asking and the amount of time the interview will probably take – so that they know what to expect. Show respect.

Give the person being interviewed control over the pace and depth of the interview. Ask for his or her permission to interview them. Explicitly reassure him or her as to their right to not answer any particular question, to take break or to discontinue the interview at any time. Let the interviewee set the pace. Give the interviewee permission to say if your questions are off target or irrelevant. Be careful about probing – ask permission. Avoid power struggles, asking questions such as 'You must tell me . . .'. Check out the interviewee's state periodically – 'How are you doing? Do you need a break?

Ensure confidentiality for the person being interviewed. Carry out the interview in a safe, private place. Be explicit regarding who else will be able to get the information from interview. Get the interviewee's explicit consent before passing information on to others. If it is impossible to ensure confidentiality, for any reason, be sure the person being interviewed knows this and consents to the interview nevertheless. Be clear with interpreters that they, too, must respect the confidentiality of the interview.

Do not rush into questions. Establish rapport before asking potentially intrusive questions. Explain fully to the person being interviewed the purpose of the interview.

Do not assume they understand the purpose just because you have told them or just because they answer 'Yes' when you ask 'Do you understand?' Ask specifically what they think the interview will accomplish.

Provide reassurance at the outset of the interview and as needed during the interview. Warn the person being interviewed that some of your questions might trigger memories or intense feelings and that these are normal reactions to retelling terrible experiences – they are not signs of being crazy, bad, sick, dirty, bewitched, etc. Observe how the person being interviewed tells their story. Be aware of shifts in body language, tone of voice conveying upset and slow down interview if necessary. Note that apparently innocuous questions or apparently innocuous aspects of the environment may trigger an intense response in a person who has been emotionally traumatized. This is especially the case with people who have been tortured or subjected to other intentional violence. Cigarette smoke, a pencil, a shirt of a particular color can remind them of the traumatic events. Educate the interviewee to be aware of his or her own triggers.

Note that mistrust of others is a common post-traumatic response to interpersonal violence. Suspiciousness and mistrust may affect the story told by the person you are interviewing. Notes taken by the interviewer may seem threatening or the person being interviewed may have fears of the consequences of telling story. In some circumstances, these fears may be very realistic. Be aware of this, reassure the interviewee, and get consent as appropriate.

A person being interviewed may tell 'different' stories at different times. This is not necessarily a sign of 'lying'. Research has shown that when a person has experienced terrifying events, memories of the event are stored in disjointed, fragmentary, emotion-laden pieces. The person who experienced the events may not have a fully coherent, linear, non-contradictory set of memories. In any case, the way they experienced the events may not entirely coincide with a 'rational', 'objective' accounting of the 'facts'. Personal truth and journalistic/legalistic truth may not coincide entirely, at least initially. This creates a potential conflict between the needs of the interviewer and interviewee. If it is irresolvable, the needs of the interviewee come first.

At the end of interview, do not abandon the person you have been interviewing. Be sure someone is available to care for them and to take them home, if needed. If material or psychological needs have been identified, give the interviewee appropriate referrals or suggest appropriate next steps. Explain how they can learn the results or other consequences of your investigation. Follow up on any implicit or explicit offers of returning, providing assistance, etc. Do not make promises you cannot keep.

Working with survivors of humanitarian emergencies

Disasters of all sorts – natural disasters, famines, accidents and 'intentional' disasters such as war or ethnic cleansing – cause great emotional pain to those directly affected by them. Direct work with individual survivors or small groups of survivors to help them recover from these emotional wounds is beyond the scope of this book. (Some sources of information about interventions with individuals and groups that are aimed specifically at helping them recover from the emotional effects of trauma are listed in Resources). But many of the day-to-day activities of humanitarian workers have a major impact on the emotional state of the direct survivors of the disaster. *The day-to-day activities of humanitarian workers may contribute enormously to the ability of the survivors to heal themselves. Or, despite the best of intentions by the aid worker, their activities may inadvertently interfere with survivors' ability to heal themselves.* Not only does this harm the individual survivors, but the emotional states of the survivors can interfere with the ability of the survivors to cooperate with the recovery project.

The most important factors determining whether people recover from the emotional impact of their traumatic experiences have to do with the environment they find themselves in after the disaster. Humanitarian workers can play a major role in creating an environment that is healing. The next section describes the kind of environment that can be healing and what you can do to help create it.

Some general principles for humanitarian work

Meet basic needs

It is difficult for people to maintain a stable emotional state, after a disaster or in any other circumstances, unless their basic needs are met.

- Survivors must be assured stable access to food, water, clothing and shelter. Poor conditions in a shelter or refugee camp – lack of food, water, sanitation, shelter; threats to personal safety – failure to provide adequate housing, uncertainty as to food and water supplies, and separation of family members from one another are themselves potent causes of emotional problems and are major obstacles to recovery from the emotional effects of the disaster.

- Needs for physical safety and security must be met. This includes protection from banditry, from the fear of looters, and from fear of rape or other assault in shelters or refugee camps.

- Survivors need assurance, if at all possible, that the disaster will not lead to the permanent loss of their land or their home. Unnecessary evacuations should be avoided. When absolutely necessary, they should be kept as short as possible.

- The safety and integrity of families must be ensured. Only in the most extreme situations should children be separated from their parents – for example, if the child's parents are abusive or rejecting because they are unable to cope with their own trauma or that of their child. If separation of a child from its parents is necessary, or if the parents have been killed or injured or are unavailable, keeping the child with another trusted adult known to them, such as a relative, a teacher, is urgent. Sending children away 'for their own protection' is almost never advisable.

■ The long term need for stable jobs, adequate housing and a functioning community must be met. Rapid physical and social reconstruction – for example, restoring or creating housing, creating jobs, reuniting families, rebuilding communities – is essential to restoring emotional equilibrium and maintaining emotional well-being at all stages of the response to disaster. At any stage of the response to disaster, failure to maintain the momentum towards meeting physical and material needs is a direct threat to emotional health.

■ Specific groups may have specific concrete needs and other specific issues may arise. For instance, women need reproductive health services and may need day care facilities for their children, even within a refugee camp. Women's safety from rape and from physical abuse at the hands of family members must be assured. Young children may have special food needs and a need for milk. People with chronic medical conditions may need to have their supplies of medication assured. Issues in refugee camps or shelters such as drug and alcohol abuse need to be addressed. Members of racial or ethnic minorities may have an especially high need for protection or for reassurance that they are safe.

Communicate

Uncertainty increases survivors' level of stress. Incorrect information produces confusion, can interfere with appropriate responses and can lead to tensions among survivors or between survivors and relief workers. Provide survivors with accurate and full information, as quickly as possible, using both individual, direct forms of communication and general public announcements – for example, via the mass media. Combat rumor mongering. It is essential to have a single source of information which survivors can rely upon – for example, a posted, regular, reliable schedule for information sharing by relief officials.

Normalize the emotional effects of disaster

While unfamiliar emotional responses are normal following a disaster, survivors may find their own reactions distressing. The best antidote is education. Reassure survivors that their responses are not a sign that they are 'going crazy'. Explain the typical time course (ie, that in most cases, symptoms can be expected to remit over a period of weeks or months). Survivors should also know that not everyone experiences the same symptoms or even any symptoms at all.

Ensure social support

Recovery from catastrophic events is inherently social. Restoring or creating networks of social support is essential in dealing with the extreme stresses created by disaster. Avoid breaking up existing communities. Combat isolation of individual survivors. Reuniting families has the highest priority. Reuniting people from the same neighborhood, work teams and other pre-existing groupings is helpful, and separating members of such pre-existing groups – and especially members of the same family – is harmful. But *beware*: reuniting neighborhoods or communities can be harmful if it entails 'reuniting' groups of people whose previous conflict is central to the humanitarian emergency – for example, different ethnic groups in a situation preceded by ethnic cleansing; different factions in a civil war.

Empower 'victims'

One of the most psychologically devastating aspects of a disaster is the victim's sense of having lost control over his or her life and fate. Interventions that help those affected by the disaster change from feeling themselves as 'victims', as passive, dependent, lacking control over their own lives, to 'survivors', who have a sense of control and confidence in their ability to cope, are central to preventing or mitigating subsequent emotional difficulties.

- Discourage passivity and a culture of dependency. Seek to engage survivors in solving their own problems.

- Survivors should be encouraged to participate in making decisions that affect their lives and to take part in implementing those decisions. They should not be denied an active role in solving problems in the interests of 'efficiency'.

- For adults, a return to work – either their usual work or other productive or personally meaningful activity – helps increase their sense of control and of competence. For children, a return to school or other structured, normalizing activity performs the same function.

Even when people must remain in a shelter for prolonged periods, developing small scale income-generating productive activities, permitting survivors to help run the shelter and the relief administration and providing skills training are useful parts of psychosocial rehabilitation.

Combat adverse community reactions

Disasters, especially intentionally created ones such as wars and ethnic cleansing, may disrupt community cohesion and may destroy the normal sense of mutual trust. One danger is that of *scapegoating*, either of individuals or using traditional divisions in the community – for example, along religious or ethnic lines. Certain groups of survivors – for example, victims of rape or those who remain permanently physically disabled – may be stigmatized. The results of the stigmatization may be as devastating as the original trauma. Active efforts to combat scapegoating and stigmatization are essential.

Avoid inadvertent re-traumatization

What appear to be trivial refugee camp or shelter rules or procedures have the potential to be re-traumatizing. For example, in cultural environments where specific rituals having to do with food preparation are expected, procedures that interfere with performance of these rituals may be a source of distress even if the food supply is entirely adequate. Or, the process of distribution of food in a shelter or refugee camp may conflict with traditional notions of who serves whom. Or the role played by humanitarian workers may seem to threaten the authority of old leaders or seem to threaten traditional parental control over children. There is no way to list all of the possible pitfalls. Sensitivity to issues such as these requires the involvement of camp or shelter residents in setting procedures.

Some cross-cultural issues

Although emotional responses to disaster are broadly similar all over the world, people from different cultural groups – including different sub-cultural groups within a larger society – may express distress in different ways and may make different assumptions about the sources of distress and how to respond to them. There are few aspects of people's experience about which they are more sensitive than their culture. Especially in times of crisis, clinging to familiar ways may help people stabilize themselves emotionally. Humanitarian workers coming from a different culture should be sensitive to these cultural needs.

How do you find out about the aspects of the culture you are working in that you need to know? How do you create services that are sensitive to local cultural patterns? One way is simply to ask the people you are working with – local staff and volunteers; local health workers, teachers, religious leaders and other community leaders; and the 'survivors' themselves – about their assumptions and needs. Another way is to involve local people in every phase of disaster services. Local health workers, priests, traditional healers, union leaders, teachers and local community leaders should be educated about the psychosocial consequences of disaster and involved in organizing aid programs. Staff members who have worked in the particular location for an extended period of time may be good guides. Finally, there may be books, articles or information you can find on the internet which may be helpful.

Some of the cross-cultural differences which you may need to take into account in interacting with people from a culture differing from you own include the following.

- Some societies explain problems, sources of stress and behavior in 'rational' or 'scientific' terms, others in more spiritual terms. Where on this continuum is the particular culture you are working with? What are the traditional ways of understanding the sources of disasters, for example, witchcraft, the will of God, fate, karma? What does this imply about expectations and needs with regard to a sense of personal control?

- How are various emotions described and expressed? Under what conditions is it socially appropriate to express emotions such as shame, guilt, fear and anger? What issues are raised by discussing feelings or practical problems in the presence of other family members?

- What are the social expectations with respect to the roles of the person directly impacted by a disaster and those helping them? What is the appropriate social distance between them? What deference is owed the helper? Are there expectations with regard to the sequences of interactions between a person seeking help and the helper? Is there an expectation that a helper will provide immediate concrete or material assistance, or direct advice or instructions?

- What is the culturally expected way of responding to terrible events? For example, it may be resignation, individual action or collective action; 'depression' may or may not be seen as a problematic way of understanding events. What are people's expectations regarding the roles played by traditional authorities, traditional healers or traditional rituals and regarding the appropriate roles of outside, 'western' experts?

- What are people's expectations with regard to authority figures and especially to those seen as representing the government?

- What rituals are important to people? Do conditions permit their observance? For instance, in some cultures, ritual ablutions (washing rituals) are engaged in every morning. Even if adequate provision is made for personal hygiene, inability to wash in the prescribed way at the prescribed time may be stressful. Failure to be able to carry out culturally required mourning or burial rituals may be especially problematic.

Note that there is no single answer to these questions. The answer may differ for different individuals or different groups – different ethnic groups, different social strata, men and women – within the community.

In any case, creating an atmosphere of trust is not merely a matter of knowing local customs and mores. Recognize that it takes two people to create a 'cross-cultural' situation. Local people as well as humanitarian workers may have a kind of dual identity, in which they behave in one way and make one set of assumptions when dealing with people from their own culture but understand that other patterns of behavior and other assumptions are needed when dealing with outsiders. It is patronizing to think that only you can be 'cross-culturally sensitive'.

At a deeper level, the relation between the cultures represented by you and the people you are trying to assist is also part of the 'cross-cultural' equation. The situations that lead to humanitarian assistance are characterized by desperate local people looking to outsiders for help in solving their problems. Coupled with doubts, instilled by a long history of colonization and foreign domination, about their own capabilities and about the value of their own culture, this can lead to self-silencing, self-marginalization and other distortions of their relationship with you.

CHAPTER 6

Going home – a journey of discovery

by John Fawcett and Amber Elizabeth Gray

'Going home' sounds simpler than 'going away,' but for many humanitarian workers, going home is the more difficult journey. Even if you were away on a short term assignment, you may face some unexpected tests. If you have been away for a much longer time, you face far greater challenges, regardless of whether your return represents a temporary withdrawal from field work – for example, to enable your children to have access to appropriate educational opportunities – or a permanent end to your work in the field. When the end of an assignment is unexpected – for example, when it follows an involuntary evacuation or other premature termination of a project – still other issues may appear. This chapter is aimed primarily at humanitarian workers who have worked for long periods of time in field environments rather than those who have completed short assignments. However, even those on short assignments will find parts of this chapter helpful. (See, especially, p. 117 on medical problems after your return and p. 121 on reconnecting with your family and friends).

At the core of a successful return home is the process of intentionally and actively determining more clearly what, exactly, 'home' means to us. 'Home' is not merely a geographical location; it is a mix of personal and social memories, experiences, expectations, culture and dreams. Our visions of 'home' change with time and experience, sometimes sharpening and sometimes fading. The longer we are away from 'home' the more this place can become idealized and fictional. It may even become unrealistic and unattainable. Even those of us who are able to maintain an objective view of home will inevitably find that over time this 'home' will have objectively changed and evolved. The basic rule for making a successful transition is to remember that while we have been away, *we* have changed as individuals, but *they* – family and friends back home – have also changed as individuals and *our culture of origin* has also changed. Nothing, in fact, has remained the same and appearances to the contrary can be deceiving. Going 'home', therefore, should always be viewed as a journey *towards* a new experience as opposed to a *return* to a previous lifestyle. It is a trip into the largely unknown, made often more confusing because many of the visual, psychological and social cues are similar to those previously experienced.

Many humanitarian workers will experience, over a career in such work, many new and different cultural and social environments. Those that have succeeded in making those multiple transitions over the years already have most of the skills and knowledge required to successfully make the transition to 'home'. Confusion and distress most often arise when we forget that this transition, too, will be made easier if we utilize the wisdom and knowledge gained over our career in humanitarian work. Remembering that this relocation is also one that requires us to 'work' at, rather than relaxing into, it will assist us to access the knowledge we need to succeed. Just as when you are facing a new assignment, when you are facing a return home, knowledge of what to expect both helps you prepare better and with less stress. This chapter seeks to examine the major components of the journey home, from the practical and logistical to the psychological and spiritual. There are, of course, many overlaps between these areas and the distinction is somewhat artificial. Breaking the components into parts may assist in creating your own process for the journey.

Some practicalities: employment, professional and insurance issues

Relocation and employment transition

For most humanitarian workers the journey home is also a process of employment transition. You may be returning home to take up positions in the head office or other home-based position with your long-term employer, or you may be leaving the employ of the agency you have worked for and may not have employment lined up in your home country, or you may be retiring from the workforce.

Regardless of the details, it is very important to make sure that your old employer has put employment transition processes in place and that any new employer is committed to providing any relocation benefits you may require. Humanitarian agencies are becoming much better at assisting in a sound relocation process for staff and families, but do not take it for granted. Check what your old and new employers will provide personally. Sometimes head office and home country divisions of humanitarian agencies are less well equipped to assist in relocations than field offices, so before leaving the field for home, try to get copies of written documents describing both the exit and re-entry provisions provided by the employing agency or agencies.

The field based agency you are leaving should provide you with a written exit document. This document should include the following elements. If it does not, use the list below as a guide when discussing transition arrangements with your agency.

Salary management processes
If you are transferring to another department within the same agency, has your salary payment been successfully transferred as well? How will you be paid? Have you already established a bank account in the new location? Will the agency assist in setting one up?

Relocation allowance
How will it be paid? If in cash, in what currency? Will it be paid into a bank account? If so, when? You will generally require larger cash amounts during relocation than at normal times.

Transportation
What and how much is covered by the agency? Will they arrange and pay for transport all the way home, or only to the nearest airport? Will they meet accommodation costs during the trip home? Will they pay for temporary accommodation at your home destination for a period while you prepare to move into your permanent home?

Shipment of personal possessions
Does the agency allow air and sea shipments? Will it help you in making arrangements? How long will you be without possessions? Are there some items you must keep with you as you move? Is there insurance coverage for shipped goods? Does this cover storage at both ends of the trip? Is the insurance company based in your new location? Or will you need to work through a third country with regard to any claims?

Health and travel insurance for yourself and your dependents
When does this end? Are there differences in the coverage you will have in your home environment? Is there advice or assistance provided for transition from the field agency's coverage to a home-based coverage?

Career counseling
Does the agency provide career transition services? Have you requested them to?

Educational issues
If you have school-age children does the agency provide assistance in finding new schools? Does it meet any education costs? If so, how are these provided?

Work references
Will the agency provide you, or prospective employers, with a work reference? Some NGO's have refused to provide such references, citing legal concerns. If this is your agency's policy, is there some way around this? For example, can you arrange to get references directly from your supervisor? Many prospective employers expect previous employers to provide references and expect applicants to ensure that such references will be available.

Professional relocation counseling services
These are not psychological or mental health services, but specialist organizations that assist international employees in going through the transition and relocation process. Many international corporations provide access to professional relocation counseling services for staff and dependents as part of employment contracts. Some NGO's are beginning to do this also, but many have not moved in this direction. It does not hurt to ask.

Tax advice
Many humanitarian workers have worked for periods in locations where personal taxation is more 'relaxed' than back home. At the same time salaries may have been paid into home-based bank accounts. Has your employer agency provided advice on potential taxation issues in your home country? It is always preferable to explore possible taxation issues prior to being visited by taxation enforcement agents. Tax authorities are less likely to 'forgive' transgressions than almost any other government body.

Legal employment issues
It is unlikely that you will encounter many legal issues relating to employment but it is a good idea to check. One area that could potentially cause concerns for humanitarian workers in future is that of legal liability. Whilst this has not, to the authors' knowledge, occurred to date, humanitarian work is in many aspects very similar to other kinds of health and welfare activities. In many western countries clients of those services have made personal damages claims against social workers, clergy, health workers and medical personnel. As humanitarian work becomes more professional, and positions itself as being professional, the clients of such work will be expecting certain standards of care and assistance. Where such

standards have not been maintained it is conceivable that legal claims could be filed against both agencies and staff. Does your present employers' insurance program meet liability claims and how could this affect you as a past employee?

Professional and educational issues

Depending on how long you have been away from home the issue as to how your professional employment experience will be regarded can become critical. Many humanitarian workers entered this field at a time when international aid was just beginning to become a profession. Highly skilled people were, at the beginning, often volunteers with minimal salaries and conditions. Today most NGO's require college or university-level qualifications, specialist skills and knowledge, and adequate professional licensure or certification. New entrants into aid work are aware of these requirements and take account of them, but those who are nearing the end of an international career and returning home may be in for a surprise as they attempt to enter the local work force.

Educational Qualifications

In the past 20 years in the highly industrialized nations, the entry-level requirements for many professions have risen considerably. A basic bachelor's degree no longer opens the door. Many professions require a specialized post-graduate degree or a Ph.D. even to get on a short-list for interviews. Although discrimination on the basis of age is prohibited in many countries, the combination of age and lack of formal educational qualifications may make obtaining employment difficult. It is essential to be aware of this before you enter the employment market. You will have to market your skills and experience instead of academic qualifications. Demonstrating a willingness to obtain required qualifications may assist, also. If possible, pursue necessary academic qualifications while you are still on international field assignment. This is, of course, difficult, but there are an increasing number of institutions that offer distance learning degrees.

■ Find out the qualification requirements for your desired profession in your home location at least two years before you expect to arrive home.

■ Investigate and utilize distance learning opportunities to upgrade your education and/or obtain educational credentials while you are still on international assignment.

■ Obtain written references from local employers and supervisors before you leave each assignment.

■ Retain copies of each of your job descriptions for future reference at home. Make a list of all the tasks you have performed at each assignment and of your accomplishments on the job. Do not rely on the formal job description to fully describe your responsibilities or activities.

■ Write your resume so that it emphasizes your experiences and responsibilities as well as your academic or professional qualifications.

Professional registration, certification or licensing processes
In many countries, most forms of teaching, social work, psychotherapy and psychological counseling, as well as other activities that relate to healthcare, mental healthcare or management and supervision of staff that have contact with clients are regulated by the government. To work in these fields requires registration, licensing or certification, which in turn, requires specific educational credentials or other specific training Practitioners may be required to engage in a program of ongoing 'continuing education' to keep their expertise current.

In some countries, registration, licensure or certification may require that you obtain police or law enforcement clearances from countries you have previously worked in. Since you may have worked in several different countries over a period of several years, this can be onerous. In addition, in some countries you may have worked in, local law enforcement agencies may either be non-existent or so limited as to make getting such clearances virtually impossible. For example, those who have worked in environments such as Afghanistan, Iraq or Kosovo may find that NATO, the UN or a 'coalition of the willing' provided the only legitimate law enforcement services. It is highly unlikely that such global institutions will provide clearance documents for individual aid workers.

- Find out whether there are any registration, certification or licensing requirements for your profession and what the relevant procedures for obtaining these credentials are, at least two years before returning home.

- Start the process of meeting registration, certification or licensing requirements well before you leave your field assignment. You may need to access or gather local information or documents as part of meeting the requirements in your home country and it is much easier to obtain this information while you are still on site.

- If there are any international organizations, institutions or even professional networks for your specialty, become a member while you are on international assignment. This may assist in home country registration.

- At each assignment location, seek out a compliant local law enforcement officer and obtain a written 'police clearance' with an official stamp. Most registration processes are seeking evidence for crimes against people – for example, child-related crimes – drugs or corruption. Retain these documents for possible use in your home country. These are virtually impossible to obtain once you have left the assignment location.

Finding employment

If you have been away for more than four or five years, the job market and application processes may have changed while you are away. The ways in which people market themselves, the role of, and accepted format for, resumes and curricula vitae and interview styles may have evolved. For instance, many employers now use internet-based pre-screening tools extensively. Knowing how to tailor your resume for this process is an acquired skill. Even the type of clothes you are expected to wear to a face-to-face interview has undoubtedly changed.

The most effective method of ensuring compliance with fashion and standards for employment processes is to make use of professional employment experts such as transition services. Large NGOs may provide access to such services for homecoming internationals. If your employer provides this benefit, take advantage of it. If your employer does not provide these services, request it. If despite your arguments, they do not see the value in providing such services, seriously consider paying for such services personally.

Whatever process you decide to use, you will find it very helpful to redraft your resume in a creative and attractive way. Long term humanitarian workers might be short on academic qualifications but will be long on experience and skills attainment. Most humanitarian work requires multi-tasking skills, lateral thinking, seat-of-the-pants decision making, crisis management, team leadership, project management, proposal writing, fund raising, cross-cultural negotiations, government and quasi-government relations, policy making, financial management and reporting, and very long working hours. You need to present your skills in a way that home-country employers can recognize and can see benefit for their own organization.

Be aware that there may be many differences between what superficially seem like similar jobs in the developing world and in the highly industrialized countries. Very few first world jobs have the complex mix of skills required by NGO workers. Professions that appear to have the same organizational status – such as managing director, for example – require significantly different skill sets in industrialized and developing world environments. A managing director in Rwanda may have to do everything from making his or her own cup of coffee, to setting up a computer network system, to answering all the e-mails that arrive, to making decisions on multi-million dollar projects, all without significant personal support. In North America or Europe such a position will have support staff, information technology specialists on call and a team of experts to assist in decision making.

There are also differences in workplace 'culture'. For example, first world managers may seem to have the luxury of more time. The 'sharpness' or urgency of humanitarian work may not be as present. Making decisions and acting on them may seem to take place at a slower pace. Decisions can often be left until tomorrow or even next week, and by 5 pm many staff will have left for home, turning off their mobile phones until the next day. It may feel that people do not really feel committed to their work and that they may seem to be merely attending work while focussing on such trivial pursuits as movies or shopping. This is in fact an unfair analysis. Living at home has as many complexities as working in front line aid work but these will be subtle and will be missed until you have developed the cultural discernment skills the locals use every day.

- Think systematically about the full range of your experiences. Identify and itemize them in a manner which you can use to show your qualifications for a job in the application or interview processes.

- Rewrite your resume/CV in the style and function appropriate to your home employment environment.

- Educate yourself about the new world of internet-based resume submission and create a resume tailored for this environment.

- Contract the services of a professional employment transition agency to assist in transition.

- Begin to train yourself to view your home employment culture as being 'different' rather than being 'slow, tedious, boring, overly complex, or irritatingly bureaucratic'. Use your extensive experience of cultural sensitivity to help you manage this process.

Arranging for healthcare and health insurance

Many humanitarian workers will find that their health has been impacted in some way during their international experience, both due to specific threats to health (discussed in Chapter 2) and to the natural results of increasing age. As the time approaches to go home, you need to evaluate your health and make decisions as to whether to pursue medical care for any existing health problems while you are still in the field or to wait until you get home. In doing so, be aware that some health problems incurred while you are on field assignment may not become evident until you return home. For instance, some infectious diseases and parasitical invasions may not be noticed until after you return home. Even chronic health problems may be attributed to the general tiredness or stress that accompanies humanitarian work as a result of difficult working and living conditions. It may only become evident that these are ongoing problems after you return.

Review your health insurance provisions very carefully before deciding whether to seek treatment before you leave your assignment or to postpone treatment until you return. Healthcare insurance provisions where you have been working may not be as comprehensive as they are at home. Alternatively, health services may be more available in your international assignment than they will be at home. Some employment-related health insurance programs enable access to some of the finest health professional services in the world. Returning home to state or poorly funded private health systems may come as a considerable shock.

Some health insurance policies will continue to cover conditions clearly related to the working conditions experienced in the field but many do not. If coverage does continue on the return home, check the policy for limitations. There may be both time limits – twelve months is common – and financial limits beyond which you will have to pay yourself. The coverage at home may be altered compared with your field cover. It is imperative to establish the link between the field environment and the medical condition prior to departing the field for full coverage to be available.

If you know you may have a medical condition that will be expensive or difficult to treat at home, it might be worthwhile considering whether it would be possible to get treatment while your employment-based health insurance is still in effect. If the procedure is serious or complex there may be implications related to work objectives and other considerations, but the longer term benefits of completing these procedures prior to arriving home might outweigh these challenges.

- Make a full assessment of your own health in the year prior to returning home.

- Think carefully about what medical conditions can be left until after you get home and which ones would be better dealt with now.

- Thoroughly review your existing health insurance policy for extensions, limitations and possible practical challenges.

- Perform a full review of the health services presently available in your home country. These have probably changed since you left.

- Have an appropriate mental health professional advise you and your accompanying family members as to the state of their stress and burnout levels.

- Review your insurance policy as it relates to psychological conditions, counseling and therapy.

Protecting your health and mental health

Medical problems after you return home

Health problems that have developed during your assignment may persist after you return home. An illness contracted in the field may be exacerbated by the physical and emotional stresses of the transition and the symptoms may worsen after your return. Or the first signs of an illness may not appear until some time after your return. In Chapter 2 we discussed signs of illnesses that are relatively common among workers who spend prolonged periods in poorer countries. Do not let down your guard yet.

When you get home, if you feel unwell or have persisting symptoms of any kind, including unusual tiredness, arrange for a thorough medical checkup. If any of your recent assignment(s) were in tropical areas, the checkup should be done by a specialist in travel medicine or tropical medicine. Whichever doctor you use, be sure he or she knows the various places you have been over the last years.

Even if you have no physical ailments or complaints, if you have been living in a developing nation for over 12 months, a checkup is advisable. And if you have any illness for which you see a doctor during the first year back home, even though you may be sure it has nothing to do with your sojourn abroad, be sure to let your physician know of your travel history.

- If you have been working in a malarial area, assume any fever in the first three or four months after your return is malaria. Sometimes the very first episode of malaria occurs only after the traveler has returned home. See a doctor immediately.

- Be wary of any fever over 39°C (102°F), or any fever at all that lasts more than three days, during the first year back home. In addition to malaria, serious illnesses characterized by fever include dengue, typhoid fever, schistosomiasis (bilharzia), sleeping sickness, typhus, meningitis, Lassa fever and hepatitis. See a doctor and inform him or her of your travel history.

- Diarrhea that persists more than 10 days after your return or that is accompanied by blood or mucus in the stool may be a sign of bacterial or amoebic dysentery or several other serious diseases. See a doctor.

- Persistent cough also merits medical advice. With the spread of AIDS, tuberculosis has become increasingly common in many countries and even though you, yourself, are not HIV-positive, it is very likely you have been exposed to TB.

Burnout and stress

Humanitarian work is emotionally and psychologically demanding and draining. Burnout, 'secondary traumatization', and other stress-related conditions lasting long after the end of an assignment are extremely common among humanitarian workers (see Chapter 4).

Regardless of whether or not you think you are suffering from the effects of stress, you should have some kind of personal psychological debriefing at the end of an assignment. The full impact of the psychological stress and chronic pressure you have experienced may not be felt until after you return home, and debriefing may help prevent any untoward effects.

A personal psychological debriefing is not the same as an operational debriefing. In the latter, the focus is on what you did in your assignments, what happened, what was done well and what not so well and what can be improved. It is aimed at improving the functioning of the agency. It also addresses the concrete and logistical needs you have in returning home – for example, the employment transition issues discussed above. In the former, the focus is on how you experienced your assignment and how you dealt with the thoughts and feelings created by your experiences. It is aimed at helping you process your experiences.

Your agency should provide both an operational debriefing and a personal psychological debriefing. The operational debriefing should come first. Not having an adequate operational debriefing is often felt as a major stressor. The pressures of making your departure make it easy to miss or skip. But an operational debriefing alone is not sufficient. You should always have a personal psychological debriefing, as well. If you have had directly traumatic experiences – for example, if you were assaulted or kidnapped or witnessed atrocities during your field assignment – it is especially urgent.

Many humanitarian agencies now provide routine end-of-contract psychological services for all employees, regardless of the employee's individual experiences or sense of need for the services. These include both a personal psychological debriefing as you make the transition and the availability of follow-up support or counseling services if you or your family should need them. If your employer does not routinely provide such services, request that they do. If your organization declines to assist, check with your health insurance company. Many health insurers do cover certain psychological services, especially if those services are preventive in nature and intent. Even if you have to arrange and pay for your own debriefing – with a counselor or mental health professional experienced in providing such debriefings – it is important to arrange it for yourself and for your accompanying family members.

Do not return home too abruptly and without the opportunity to prepare yourself for the transition. With the ease inherent in modern air travel, it is possible to leave your assignment location in the morning and to be walking into your relatives' house in your home country in the afternoon. The transition time frame is so short that there is very little opportunity to build the psychological strength you need for the transition. If at all possible, arrange to create a transition space, even at the risk of upsetting family and friends. Giving yourself a day or two to pause en route home provides a physical and psychological breathing space between the leaving and arriving. It helps you leave your old life well and return home well prepared for your new life. This is especially important if your return home was unanticipated – for example, as a result of an emergency evacuation or other premature termination of the project you were working on.

- Arrange for both an operational debriefing and a personal psychological debriefing at the end of your assignment, before you return home.

- Consider building in a transition period between departing the field location and arriving home. Try to choose a location that is restful and that will provide services you may require. Try to arrange for a debriefing or other mental health consultation during the transition period.

Home at last: reintegrating and reconnecting

Reverse culture shock

Returning home may result in more culture shock than you experienced when you first entered a developing country. You left home with a sensory and psychological picture of your home country, based on your prior experience of it. Over the course of time, that picture becomes increasingly fictional. Over time, cultures and societies, even your own, change. Your original experience was personal and was set in a particular time and place. Your view of that time and place becomes more idealized – not necessarily positively – as the time since you lived there grows. You have been forced to rethink the 'meaning' of home as you have compared it with the increasing variety of environments you have lived in over the intervening years. Both you and 'home' have changed. The 'home' you left no longer exists, if indeed it ever did.

The Humanitarian Companion

When you return home you will find the signs and signatures of a global culture, just as you have in your field assignments. Your own culture of origin may be thriving and continuing to develop, but it will have altered since you departed and will have been impacted by forces from abroad. The population demographics will have changed and political alliances will have altered. The names of key social, political and community leaders will be different. Colors and designs will have evolved. Roads may no longer go where they used to, or will now go places they did not used to. Financial services will have changed and your old bank may not be the best anymore. Communication systems will have undoubtedly changed, but sometimes not as fast as in the field environments you have served in. Legal requirements may have changed, or your perceptions of them altered with time. What seemed to be a secure and supportive environment years ago now may be experienced as controlling, invasive and repressive. You may need to obtain permission for activities that are done 'freely' in emergency relief situations.

Other behaviors you observe may appear overly permissive and offensive when compared with more controlled countries. Gender roles and attitudes towards various patterns of sexual behavior may have changed. You may be put off by what seems to be excessive materialism or feel that your values and the values of your home society have diverged. After your time with a very diverse international group of people – both colleagues and recipients of assistance – you may find people at home seem very provincial or very uniform. It may seem hard to have meaningful discussions about your experiences with people who do not even know the location of the countries in which you have worked. You are very likely to think that the youth of today are different – worse, more selfish, less respectful, less concerned with values, etc. – than they were when you were young. This may have little to do with your international experience and more to do with your age. However, the reality is that you have probably missed the evolutionary processes that have influenced all age groups while you have been overseas.

At the same time, it is easy to exaggerate the real changes that have occurred at home. It is true that the world has become a smaller, more intimate place, with global trends, fashions and information impacting local cultures in ways not seen before. It is a mistake, however, to assume that all cultures have become the same or that your home culture has become more 'American' or more 'European' or even more globally homogenous. Cultures are surprisingly resilient and retain more strength than was previously thought possible. Despite the fact that CocaCola and Nike can be purchased in almost every country, the underlying cultural foundations have remained. Local cultures tend to interpret global trends, rather than adopt them without analysis. While the ingredients may be the same, the 'cappuccino culture' of the US Pacific Northwest is not the same as that found in London, England or Dakar, Senegal. People all over the world may wear Manchester United shirts but the 'red army' of Thailand is not the same as that found in the English midlands on a Saturday afternoon.

Before going home, prepare yourself for your home culture.

- Read on-line home newspapers while you are on assignment. Read not only the news sections but the social and entertainment pages as well.

- Have home magazines sent to your assignment location. Read the advertisements as well as the articles. Look at the photos of houses, people, clothing and urban landscapes. This will prepare you for any overall structural changes.

- Check out information on recent fiction and non-fiction written in your home country, on films, on music and on plays. These provide significant insight into local cultural themes and changes.

- Keep an occasional eye on home politics. If you can vote from overseas do so. The sense of ownership gained through electoral processes assists in the transition home.

- Try to follow home country sporting action. Even if you are not a sports fan remember that when you return home, people will be using sports as a major conversation item.

- Watch out for information relating to changes in legal issues in your home country, particularly those relating to social security, pension and taxation issues. If there are pre-requisites for access to government benefits, find out what they are before you return home. For example, if you are expecting to receive a government retirement benefit on returning home, check whether there is a minimum residency or contribution period. The law may have changed to require that you work for a minimum period of time in the home country immediately prior to retirement.

- Check out whether there have been any banking changes over the years. How are credit limits established and measured? Are you still eligible for credit cards, loans, mortgages or other bank services? Is it possible to establish a sufficient banking record well before you return home to reduce possible transition problems?

- Find out if driver's license rules or procedures have changed. Is your present license suitable for driving at home? How do you go about obtaining a home license and is there anything you can do to enhance that process before you leave your assignment?

- If you are a US citizen or permanent resident who left the country before September 11, 2001, check whether there are any new Homeland Security documentation or registration requirements that were not in place before you left the USA.

Reuniting with friends and family

Returning home is an opportunity to reconnect with family members and friends but, in your time away, everybody has grown and changed and, as a consequence, relationships need to be reformed. Your family members may have difficulty reconnecting with you, just as you may have with them.

In your family of origin people will have aged. Some may have died, others may have married and new children may have been born. Some of your family may never have met you and some may not even have heard of you. Family members with whom you had significant relationships prior to your departure overseas may have formed stronger and more relevant relationships with other family members or with people outside the extended family. Your family may have restructured its relationships to include you as an absent member. Their whole relationship with you may now be defined by communication via email or telephone.

Now that you are present physically, you occupy a different space in the relationship network. This can take some time to work out. Over the years the topics of conversation and what is permitted to be openly discussed compared with that which is now taboo, may well have changed. In some conversations you will feel like a complete stranger or as if you are being treated as an outsider. You and your family will need time to develop the relationships based on where everyone is today, not where they were a decade ago. To your family, it is the changes in you that are most obvious. To them, any assumption you make that everything is as it was before you left may be jarring at best, infuriating to the point of being intolerable at worst.

Even after short stays abroad, returning to your family can be surprisingly complicated. You may be looking forward to being greeted with open arms upon your return, but others in your family may have resented your absence or may have become used to being independent of you. What was all gain to you may be, at least in part, loss to them. For you, it is your own experiences that seem exciting and important. For family members, their having had to deal with a broken washing machine, a child's sickness or other minor family crises may be more salient. To you, your family's apparent lack of interest in your experiences seems insulting; to them, your lack of interest in what was important to them seems yet another abandonment.

Try to prepare your family for your return before you actually arrive. It may be helpful to send them a copy of this section of this manual and the preceding section – on 'reverse culture shock'. It will help them understand better what you are going through.

One issue that may complicate coming home to your family and friends are differences in expectations about communicating experiences and feelings. Some humanitarian workers may be less equipped to verbally share intense or deep emotional or spiritual experiences than others. Within the international humanitarian community much is intuitively understood and agreed to without any need to discuss it explicitly. Your fellow workers and the family next door, even if they work for another NGO or a religious mission, share essentially the same world and are affected by the same trends and events. Your individual experiences may be intense and deeply felt, but there is little need to talk about these experiences in order to be understood. In other humanitarian situations, you may have worked in an environment that provides a strong social support system, encourages people to take advantage of counseling opportunities and provides training in interpersonal skills. As a result, you may have become very expert at sharing deeply held feelings and experiences.

Regardless of which end of the spectrum your own experience falls, you face challenges when you return home. If you have not developed strong abilities to talk about your experience and your reactions to it, you may find yourself feeling angry that your friends and family members do not seem to intuitively understand what you are experiencing or when to intervene. If you do have good skills at talking about your experience, you may find that home-based colleagues and family members seem unwilling or unable to enter into the kind of 'deep' conversations you are used to. Remember that the use of interpersonal skills to explore deeply held feelings is connected strongly with appropriate context. Many people who live in Western cultures often see the appropriate context for intense sharing as being more formal environments, such as 'support groups' or counseling/therapy relationships. But going home can be an excellent opportunity to develop strong relationships with friends and family based on the life experiences of both the returnee and those at home.

- Ask a close family member to give you an updated family tree with names, birthdays, geographical location, etc. This will help you and your children identify who is connected to whom.

- Be aware that family members have changed and grown with the years. When you get home, take plenty of time to listen to relatives and friends to find out how they have changed and grown. Be careful not to criticize or offer advice until you are sure you have the full picture. Do not assume you can step into exactly the same roles and same patterns of behavior as before.

- Assess your interpersonal communications skills and style. Can you talk about your experiences, including emotional experiences, in a 'deep' way? Identify the people at home with whom you would like to develop or deepen close relationships. Do their expectations about sharing experiences and feelings match yours? Consider paying for a few training sessions on relationship skills, either before you return home or at home. This could sharpen your ability to relate well to those you wish to communicate with.

- Do not assume that people are uninterested in you. Most family relationships are actually made up of a long series of apparently trivial communications. Over time, however, these communications form the strong web that is 'family', and allow more deep and meaningful discussions to occur in an environment of trust. Cultivate patience and focus on the small and the immediate. The rest will come with time.

- Major experiences in your life may not be immediately interesting to others. On the other hand, major experiences in theirs may not be interesting to you. Most people, in fact, do not spend a lot of time talking about historical major experiences but live in the present. Again, cultivate patience, and when the time does come for remembrance, be prepared to listen as well as talk.

■ Every family has its store of 'myths'. Myths are tales that may or may not be objectively accurate but are very powerful nonetheless. You may be one of those myths yourself. People do not often talk specifically about myths. The mythical power often lies in the unspoken but shared nature of the epic. This may make it more difficult for you to have conversations about your international experiences.

■ Your re-entry into your family will be greatly facilitated by appropriate preparation.

Before you leave for your field assignment, ask a close family member or friend to keep all correspondence – letters, e-mails – you send him or her and to return them to you when you return. Having one person serve as a guardian of your thoughts and experiences, as reflected in your writing, can provide a sense of continuity and connection and support and contact throughout the transition.

Keep a journal that you begin as soon as you are hired and record the process of preparing to leave for your new assignment, your time spent on the assignment and the transitions to and from home and the assignment. Reviewing and rereading these writings can give you a sense of the continuities in your experience that can support your connection to all phases of the process.

Ask someone at home to agree to regular and consistent communication with you, whether it is a weekly phone call, e-mail or letter.

Reintegrating children into the family

Family reintegration may be particularly challenging for your own children if they were with you on assignment. Many humanitarian workers enter the international work force with relatively young children and return home, years later, with teenagers for whom they wish to provide sound high school education. Some of these children may have no memories of a previous life and their views of 'home' may be a distorted version, formed from your own reports and conversations. Family members who you meet enthusiastically may be complete strangers to your children and similarly aged relatives may appear to be from a completely different culture.

Expatriate communities in humanitarian environments tend to be fairly close and small in numbers. Often very close relationships are formed by children of humanitarian workers at international or mission schools and these relationships are much more important than those with distant relatives only dimly remembered. Teenage children returning home often feel completely isolated and even abandoned as their parents enter into a busy social time and the children are left to face different and often frightening school experiences.

Anything that can reduce the element of surprise and apprehension, especially for children, is worth doing. To assist children making the re-entry to home, consider using a professional transition agency. If your employer is unable to fund such a service, you may want to make use of one personally. An increasing number of publications are also available from global on-line booksellers on this topic. It is best to begin reading and studying this transition well before making the actual move.

- Locate resources relating to children returning home if you have children making this transition.

- If you have a family with you, begin the process of discussing family dynamics and family history. Many things you take for granted may be unknown to your children.

- Identify ways in which you and your family can retain communication links with friends made at the overseas location. Some of these relationships could prove to be life-long. The possibility of losing close friends and being isolated in a new environment can be especially unsettling to children.

- If you have school age children, find out about the local school they will be likely to attend before leaving for home. It may be helpful to connect your children with a teacher or administrator at the school, via e-mail, before you return. Remember, however, that being part of a group and conforming to local social norms is very important teenage behavior. Try not to make your teenagers stand out from the crowd.

- Be aware that educational systems change over time. Examinations that you thought important when you were younger may not even exist any more. New ones may have arisen to replace them. Curricula may have changed. Try to learn what these changes have been, even before you return. The internet and communications with friends and family back home can help.

- Educational culture and ways of learning differ between countries. International schools often mix such cultures, but not all do. School years also differ significantly, especially between the Northern and Southern hemispheres. Prepare at least one full school year in advance in order for your children to make the transition as easily as possible.

- Entrance into tertiary (university) level education carries with it specific requirements, but these differ between countries. It may be that the school in the country of assignment does not offer a way to obtain entrance to university level study at home. (There are agencies in the USA and Europe that, for a fee, will 'translate' educational experiences earned abroad into a version acceptable at home. Colleges and universities in your home country can direct you to these agencies). Try to work with educational authorities in order to maximize opportunities to access such education. It can be extremely hard to go back in time and gain qualifications that those at home have automatically received. This can be particularly challenging in the USA but other countries can be challenging as well.

Coming to terms with your sense of purpose, spirituality and religion

People enter international humanitarian work for a wide variety of reasons. Most often this decision rests on a mix of secular values and ethics, and religious and spiritual concerns: 'To make a difference, to save the children, to transform human experience, to be the hands and feet of God'. For some, motivation rests on a well-formulated theology or philosophy. For others, it stems from more of a strong 'feeling' that 'something should be done'. Still others drift into humanitarian work and later look back with wonder as to how they got there in the first place.

Whatever your original motivation for becoming a humanitarian worker, front-line field experiences always challenge your reasons for being there. It is impossible to be involved in humanitarian work and not come face to face with both deep evil and surprising good. The bad that human beings do to each other appears to be often surpassed by the unfairness of the world or of God. Yet, the most unexpected generosity can arise from the most unexpected sources, giving rise to hope and even joy.

The day-to-day challenges and pressures of humanitarian work and the changes over time in the humanitarian mission itself (see Ch. 1, pp. 13–16) require you to examine and re-examine the beliefs and hopes you left home with. Your original motivations may collapse under the weight of new evidence or hard challenges. You may need to form and adopt new reasons for staying or going on to another assignment. Old reasons may be refined, strengthened and affirmed through your life in the field. Whatever the outcome, the process is often a combination of intense emotional, physical and psychological pressures.

It is not surprising therefore that many humanitarian workers return home after a career in humanitarian aid work with a strong sense of why they did what they did. Others may have a deep sense of their own failure to understand why they did what they did. It is unusual to find a career humanitarian or mission worker who is ambivalent about their life's work at the end of it. Whether your initial motives were affirmed or destroyed, your feelings about your work are likely to be deeply held and often very intensely self-analyzed.

The challenge when you get home is how to articulate the positions you have arrived at without alienating those who saw you depart. A significant factor in the life of humanitarian aid workers is the fact that theirs is most often a shared experience. As you have gone through your various assignments, your colleagues and family members have had to face and deal with fairly similar challenges. Even when these experiences have not been openly shared or discussed, the very nature of the work creates a kind of loose community within a global context. The stories that are told come out of a background of similar assumptions, beliefs and experiences.

When you return home, it may seem to you that your friends and family members at home have not experienced such an intense refining of their sense of purpose, and it is possible that they have not. You may experience those greeting you as shallow, lacking depth and wisdom, fickle in their opinions. In return, home country friends might find you a little too 'intense', too 'serious', 'not able to relax and enjoy'. In reality, both perceptions are inaccurate and unhelpful. All human beings go through intense emotional, psychological or spiritual experiences in life. A person does not need to be an aid worker to experience a deep search for meaning or relevance. Development of identity, coping with loss and grief, meeting challenges to your faith and belief are a significant part of everyday life and not merely the provenance of the humanitarian profession.

Conflicts over identity and your sense of meaning and purpose may be an especially complex issue for staff of Christian or other religious agencies whose livelihood has often depended on supporters or donors at home who share similar religious backgrounds. Over the years you may have been required to spend time in your home country marketing the program you are working in order to raise funds to keep it going. In order to do this, you may have had to steer clear of potentially controversial matters and focus on the clear and relatively simple. Complexity does not generally assist in raising funds. This can create a stressful dichotomy for the worker. In front of the donor community you must appear to have the same beliefs as when you left for the field, but this may conflict with the often extensive and painful personal growth and development you have experienced in the course of carrying out the work. While it is often possible to put on a publicly acceptable face while you are still in service, when you return home at the end of an assignment or a career, it is more difficult to do so. Admitting to significant changes in belief, theology, religious behavior or values may shock your home community and disrupt or sever relationships. The financial pressures are now lifted but the social pressures remain. Yet for the sake of your own integrity, the truth must be told.

The pressure may be less sharply focused for workers who were not part of a mission-based agency, but it still can be troubling. You have undergone spiritual or philosophical or religious transformations not necessarily shared by even your closest friends back home. When you return, you may feel misunderstood, estranged, spiritually and emotionally alone.

Begin preparing for such challenges early in your assignment or career. Try to maintain or develop a small group of peers, colleagues or friends with whom you can share your own sense of anguish, exultation, exploration, personal growth and change in an ongoing way. This network will become your closest source of professional support and may overlap with the group of your closest, deepest friends. Ideally, many of this group will actually reside in your home country and will be part of the community you return to. This establishes a link between the beginning and ending of your work and enables your transition process to take place within the context of ongoing relationships. For many humanitarian workers, however, your support group consists of a widely scattered group of friends who have a tacit understanding of each other's experiences and feelings. You may not be in close physical proximity, but your 'spiritual' proximity is what can be most important and valuable.

- Why did you enter humanitarian work? Did you have a religious or spiritual reason?

- Are your motivations for humanitarian work now the same as they were when you started? Are your spiritual or religious beliefs the same? How have they changed and why?

- Will any changes in your belief system, religious behavior or your understanding of the nature of human beings shock or surprise those at home? How much does this matter to you? Are there financial, social or institutional considerations connected to this surprise?

- When you consider the lives of those at home, seek to understand at what points they, too, faced significant issues of life and death, of meaning and loss, or spiritual crisis and growth.

- Reflection on the tasks of different phases of life is appropriate as part of making your transition. Developmental tasks such as starting a family or spending time with aging parents may take on a new meaning and priority following years in the field.

- Finding channels for 'giving back' to your community at home may help ease the transition, both by helping reintegrate you into your community and by establishing a concrete link between the values you have developed and the life you are redeveloping at home.

- As you have grown and developed have you shared this journey with anyone, or with a group or network of friends or colleagues? It is not too late to begin. It is most effective if you have close companions already in the home environment as well as where you are at present. If you have experienced changes, have you considered how these might be articulated appropriately? Which venue, or what network or group would be supportive as you go through this reentry process?

Conclusion

Going home can be the most exciting part of the humanitarian experience. Now is the time when you connect all you have learned and experienced and achieved, all you have lost and failed at and become disappointed with, with your home community. This is the opportunity to reflect on what called you out and to consider what calls you back. Along the way you will have discarded some aspects of your life and picked up many more. You will have skills and expertise that will be valuable to your home country and your extended family for years to come. As you utilize all your knowledge of how to manage transitions, you will gain a new appreciation of those who remain your 'family' and of the culture and context that has always been your 'home'. If you enter this process with the same degree of commitment you showed when you headed out on assignment you will succeed and find pearls of great value and enjoyment. Another assignment, another country, and this time the one called 'home.'

Resources

The 'before you go' checklist

Tasks

- See your doctor ☐
  - Obtain necessary immunizations ☐
  - Begin malaria prophylaxis* ☐
  - Get first aid training, or refresh your knowledge ☐

- Check, or remind yourself of, your blood type ☐

- See your dentist ☐

- Check health insurance coverage ☐

- Make or review will and arrange or review a power of attorney ☐

- Pay outstanding bills ☐

- Arrange for payment of ongoing bills ☐

- Arrange for mail forwarding ☐

- Leave copy of travel itinerary and contact information
  with family or friends ☐

- Miscellaneous, for example, arrange pet care, discontinue
  newspaper delivery ☐
  - _____ ☐
  - _____ ☐
  - _____ ☐

Pack

- Small bag or backpack ☐

- Clothes: 4–5 changes ☐

- Dress-up clothes (one set) ☐

- Shoes (closed) ☐

- Outer garments (coat, raincoat, etc.) ☐

- Towel and facecloth ☐

- Toiletries:
  - shampoo ☐
  - soap ☐
  - toilet paper ☐
  - facial tissues ☐
  - brush and comb ☐
  - razor and shaving soap ☐
  - toothbrush ☐
  - toothpaste ☐
  - floss ☐
  - nail clippers ☐
  - liquid clothes detergent ☐
  - contact lens cleaning supplies ☐
  - lip balm ☐
  - vitamins ☐
- Electrical equipment (_____) ☐
- Electrical converters and plug adaptors, if needed ☐
- Stationery ☐
- Sunscreen (SPF 30) ☐
- Hat with brim ☐
- Insect repellent (25–30% DEET) ☐
- Mosquito net impregnated with insecticide ☐
- Extra insecticide for re-soaking mosquito net ☐
- Medical supplies:
  - Prescription medications ☐
  - Antibiotics ☐
  - Over the counter medications ☐
  - Allergy medication ☐
  - Analgesic (aspirin, acetaminophen/paracetamol, ibuprofen) ☐
  - Anti-diarrhea medication ☐
  - Anti-fungal ☐
  - First aid kit ☐
  - Needle and syringe kit* ☐
  - Sterile lancet* ☐
  - Needle and suture kit, IV-giving set, IV fluid* ☐
  - Epinephrine auto-injector kit* ☐
- Spare glasses or contact lenses and copy of eyeglass prescription ☐
- Personal hygiene items:
  - Tampons ☐
  - Contraceptives ☐
  - Miscellaneous ☐

The Humanitarian Companion

- Water purification tablets or kit ☐

- Travel documents:
  - Passport ☐
  - National identity card (if applicable) ☐
  - Visa/work permits ☐
  - Organizational id card ☐
  - Driver's license ☐
  - Medical insurance card ☐
  - Yellow fever immunization certificate ☐
  - Tickets ☐
  - Letters of introduction ☐
  - Extra passport-size photos ☐
  - Photocopies of all documents ☐

- Money, credit cards, travelers checks, personal checks, as needed ☐

- Water bottle or canteen ☐

- Reference materials ☐

- Miscellaneous (for example, • calculator, • computer/modem,
  • cassette or cd player, • books, • cards, • board games, • binoculars,
  • camera, film and batteries, • other hobby supplies) ☐

- 'Carry on' luggage contains at least one change of clothes
  and basic toiletries ☐

* If appropriate, based on where you are going and your particular individual
  medical needs.

RESOURCE II

First Aid: a brief manual

Preliminaries: 'DR ABC'
    D is for Danger
    R is for Response
    Assessing airway
    Assessing breathing
    Assessing circulation; CPR

Assessing and responding to other problems
    Bleeding
    Shock
    Burns
    Fractures
    Heat stroke and heat exhaustion
    Hypothermia and frostbite
    Animal, snake and insect bites and stings

Most medical conditions you encounter in the field are not immediately life threatening. The few that are can generally be addressed by anyone with basic first aid skills and a rational approach. Try to remain calm and thoughtful. Panic will interfere with your own ability to act, may contribute to a 'shock' response in the victim, and may cause others to act irrationally, as well.

WARNING: There is a definite risk to the first aid responder from the bodily fluids of the victim. These include blood, mucus, urine and other secretions. You should take the steps necessary to protect yourself before attempting to treat the patient. Use surgical gloves, if you have them. There should be a pair in your first aid kit. If you give mouth-to-mouth resuscitation, use a cardiopulmonary resuscitation barrier device. A facemask will also reduce the potential for rescuer infection.

Preliminaries: DR ABC

The most urgent elements in responding to emergency situations are summarized by the acronym DR ABC. Remember them and use them as a checklist for first responses in any emergency.

D is for Danger

You cannot help the victim if you get injured or killed on the way or if the victim is in immediate danger of further injury. Determine whether or not you can safely and effectively render assistance. Check for traffic, ongoing sources of electrical shock, land mines or other hazards. Moving the victim can make their injury worse, so do *not* move the victim unless you absolutely have to for your safety or for theirs – for example, if there is an immediate threat to the victim, such as traffic. This advice is especially urgent if there is even the slightest possibility that the victim suffered a head, neck, or back injury – for example, if there is bleeding from nose, mouth, or ears.

R is for Response

When you arrive at the victim's side, ask 'Are you all right?' There is no need to shake the victim to gain a response. Their response gives you immediate information. If the victim can answer, you already know that they are conscious and breathing and that their heart is working. A victim that does not react should be considered unconscious.

Go on to assess the most immediately life threatening aspects of their injury, the 'ABCs': airway – make sure that the victim's airway is open; breathing – check that the victim is breathing; and circulation – check for signs of circulation.

Airway

If a person's airway is obstructed, they will be unable to speak or breathe. If they are coughing or gasping strongly for air, leave them alone. *Do not slap* them on the back. If the obstruction is at the entrance to the trachea, then reactions to the slaps may cause the person to inhale the object and cause complete obstruction. If the person is unable to speak, trying to clear their throat or coughing weakly, stay with them and carefully monitor their breathing.

If the victim is unable to speak and puts their hands around their throat, act promptly: this is the universal sign for choking. Clearing the airway is easiest if the patient is standing. Stand behind the patient. Make a fist with one hand and place it over the patient's abdomen, thumb side toward the patient, between their navel and the bottom of their rib cage. With your other hand, grasp your wrist. With a sharp inward and upward thrust, compress the abdomen. Repeat until the airway is clear. If the victim is unconscious or too large for you to get your arms around, lay them on their back. Position your palm on the victim's forehead and gently push backward, placing the second and third fingers of your other hand alongside the side of the victim's jaw, tilting the head and lifting the chin forward to open the airway. Remove any obviously visible obstruction from the victim's mouth. Do not take any appreciable time to do this and do not do a routine finger sweep if you do not immediately see the obstruction. It is better to quickly start chest compressions, which will generate enough pressure to remove any foreign bodies still there. Use an abdominal thrust with both hands similar to a CPR chest compression (see below).

Breathing

If the victim is unconscious, check for breathing. This evaluation procedure should take only three to five seconds. If the victim is not breathing or you are in doubt, start artificial respiration immediately. Look to see if their chest rises. Put your ear directly over their mouth to listen and to feel for air being expelled. Listen for coughing. Feel for the rise of the chest.

If the victim is not breathing, kneel and position yourself at a right angle to the victim's body, with your knees perpendicular to the victim's neck and shoulders. Pinch the victim's nose closed, using your thumb and forefinger. Take a deep breath. Open your mouth wide and place it tightly over the victim's mouth and exhale slowly and gently into the victim. Repeat. Check to see that the victim's chest is rising when you exhale. If the stomach bulges, instead, the air is going into the victim's stomach and not into their lungs, which suggests their airway is obstructed (see above).

Circulation

Look for signs of circulation. These include breathing, coughing, signs of movement or coughing in response to the rescue breaths, swallowing, warmth or skin color. *Do not waste time looking for a pulse*: studies show that it usually takes too much time and is an inaccurate way of assessing circulation.

If the victim shows signs of circulation but is still not breathing, continue mouth-to-mouth resuscitation, using big breaths every five seconds (12 times per minute). Continue to check for signs of breathing and watch for chest breaths. If the victim's breathing is weak, you may have to continue mouth-to-mouth resuscitation, following the victim's breathing pattern but ensuring a breath at least every five seconds.

If there are no signs of circulation, or you are at all unsure, begin cardiopulmonary resuscitation (CPR). Although training is helpful in preparing you to administer CPR, the indications for CPR are that the patient is unconscious, not breathing and with no signs of circulation. Death is imminent. Under these circumstances, any resuscitation is better than no resuscitation.

To restore circulation you must begin heart compressions. Kneel and position yourself at a right angle to the victim's chest. Find the base of the breastbone and the center of the chest where the ribs form a 'V'. Position the heel of one hand on the chest immediately above the V. With the other hand, grasp the first hand from above, intertwining the fingers. Shift your weight forward and upward so that your shoulders are over your hands. Straighten your arms and lock your elbows. Shift your weight onto your hands to depress the victim's chest 4–5 cm (11/2–2 inches) in an adult or older child. Count aloud as you repeat for a total of fifteen chest compressions, in an even rhythm, slightly faster than one compression per second (100 beats per minute). Alternate pumping and breathing (mouth-to-mouth resuscitation). Pump the victim's chest 15 times, then breathe for him or her twice. Establish a regular rhythm, counting aloud. Stop to re-check for signs of a circulation after 1 minute, and then every 2 minutes. Also stop to check if the casualty makes a movement or takes a spontaneous breath.

Continue until help comes, if possible.

> *Note.* If you are unable or unwilling to perform both chest compression and breathing, just do the compressions, at a rate of about 100 compressions per minute. Many people do not perform CPR or delay in starting it because they are reluctant to do mouth-to-mouth breathing. Some recent studies have found that survival rates for standard CPR and chest-compressions-only are about the same. If you will breathe and you can breathe, you should breathe. But doing something is much better than doing nothing.

CPR on a child. The procedure is essentially the same, but use only one hand for chest compressions (1/3 the depth of the chest in a child under the age of 8). Pump five times, then breathe once for the child, breathing more gently than you would for an adult. Compressions should be at about 100 per minute for children, at least 100 compressions a minute for infants.

Two person CPR. If two people are available to provide first aid, one person provides a breathing assistance while the other pumps the heart. Pump the heart at about 100 beats per minute. After every fifteen compressions, a pause in pumping is allowed for two breaths to be given by the other person. The two first aiders should work from opposite sides of the victim. Note that if two people are available to give CPR, the first priority is for one of them to summon help. One person should go for help while the other starts one-person CPR.

Assessing and responding to other problems

Once you know that the ABCs are okay, you can move on to assessing what other urgent problems the victim may have. Look for (a) bleeding; (b) shock; (c) chemical or thermal or electrical burns; (d) fractures; (e)heat exhaustion or heat stroke; (f) frostbite or hypothermia; and (g) animal, snake and insect bites and stings.

Bleeding

There are several ways to control bleeding. These should be attempted in the following order.

1 Using a sterile gauze square, apply pressure directly over the wound. When it stops bleeding, tape or otherwise secure the gauze in place. Note that immediately removing the gauze may cause the bleeding to restart.

2 If you have knowledge of the arterial pressure points, apply pressure, using one or both thumbs over the artery. Once this has controlled the bleeding, apply a pressure bandage to the wound itself.

3 If you are unable to control the bleeding of a limb in any other way and professional help is many hours away, apply a tourniquet to the affected extremity. *This is a last resort*, to be undertaken only in cases of severe, otherwise uncontrollable and life-threatening bleeding. There is a high risk of losing the extremity, particularly if professional attention is not available immediately.

Bleeding from the torso does not lend itself to control by any method other than direct pressure. Ice applied to the wound causes the vessels to contract and may help control bleeding. With a bleeding limb, elevation of the limb and ice may help. Bleeding from the head can usually be controlled by direct pressure, elevation, icing or a combination of the three. Do not apply a tourniquet.

Shock

The most commonly encountered form of shock in the field is traumatic shock, induced by an injury. If left untreated, it may result in death. Always monitor the patient for signs of shock and routinely treat it in cases of severe injury. The patient may be cold and clammy, have pale skin, a rapid weak pulse, shallow or irregular breathing, complain of dizziness or weakness, show evidence of confusion or a combination of these symptoms. Except in case of head injury, have the patient lie flat on their back and elevate their legs. Cover them with a blanket or other thermal cover and monitor the ABCs.

Burns

There are three major types of burn: chemical, electrical and thermal. The treatment for each is different but in every case, treatment for traumatic shock should be part of your approach.

Chemical burns may arise from inadvertent spills when handling chemicals, coming in contact with improperly disposed of chemicals and chemical wastes, or chemical warfare acts. Take precautions to ensure that you are not yourself contaminated or exposed to the chemical before attempting treatment. If you can determine the nature of the chemical that caused the burn, it will be helpful in determining a course of treatment. Remove all contaminated clothing. Thoroughly rinse the exposed areas with copious amounts of clean, lukewarm water for at least 20–30 minutes (longer, if possible). Seek professional medical attention as soon as possible, regardless of the apparent severity of the burn.

Electrical burns usually result from electrical shock. Before approaching the patient, be certain that no further risk of injury is present. If you know the patient is still in contact with the electrical source and you know it is low voltage, you can move the wire or the patient to a safe position with a dry pole or rope. If the wire is *unknown or high voltage*, get professional help to shut off the current or move the wire. Attempting to do so yourself will likely result in an increase in the body count for this accident. Do not do it.

As soon as it is safe to do so, check the ABCs and continue to monitor them. Patients with electrical shock often suffer cardiac arrest or respiratory arrest. If there are evident burns, cover them loosely with a sterile dressing. Seek professional help in treating the burns. Do *not* apply burn creams or ointments.

Thermal burns range from mild sunburn to the severe burns associated with open flames and heated metal. Thermal burns are categorized by degree. Appropriate treatment is keyed to the severity of the burn.

First degree burns are characterized by minor swelling and redness of the affected area. Apply cool running water or wet compresses as soon as possible, continuing until the pain subsides. Leave the burned area exposed. Do *not* apply ointments or salves. If pain recurs, reapply cold water.

Second degree burns are characterized by redness of the affected area, swelling and blisters. Treat as above for first degree burns for 15–30 minutes, using sterile water. Do not break blisters or use ointments or salves. Cover with a dry, sterile bandage. Elevate the burned area and treat the patient for traumatic shock. Seek professional help.

Third degree burns are typically areas of deeper burning, surrounded by areas that show the characteristics of second degree burns. Charring or a leathery appearance are common. Check the ABCs and continue to monitor them. Treat for traumatic shock. Leave burned clothes on skin. If skin is bare, cover the burned area with a dry, sterile, non-adhesive dressing. Elevate the burned area. Seek professional help immediately.

Fractures

Usually the patient will know if they have broken a bone. The symptoms are bruising around the fracture site, localized pain, deformity and swelling. Immobilize any fracture before moving a patient. This is especially important in the case of known or suspected neck or spinal injury. In treating a fracture, the object is to immobilize the ends of the broken bone. When splinting a fracture, immobilize the adjacent joints as well as the fracture site. After splinting is completed, check circulation in the extremities. Continue to do so until professional help is obtained. In the case of an open fracture – where the bone is exposed and visible – you will most likely need to control the bleeding using pressure points instead of direct pressure.

Heat stroke and heat exhaustion

Heat stroke occurs when the body is unable to regulate its own temperature. The patient will have hot, dry skin and a temperature well above normal – above 39°C or 103°F. There may also be headache, a rapid pulse, dizziness, nausea, confusion or unconsciousness. This is a life-threatening situation and must be treated immediately and aggressively. You must immediately lower the body temperature or it is very likely that the patient will die. Get the patient out of the sun and into a cool space. Remove their clothing and immerse them in cool, *not* icy, water – or sponge them with cool water and fan them – until the onset of shivering. Seek medical attention.

Heat exhaustion is a milder heat-related illness that can develop after several days of exposure to high temperatures and inadequate or unbalanced replacement of fluids. Warning signs include heavy sweating, clammy skin, paleness, muscle cramps, tiredness, weakness, dizziness, headache, nausea or vomiting ands fainting. Get the patient out of the direct sun and cool them down with cold compresses, a cool shower or bath or sponge bath and fanning. If they are conscious, give oral rehydration fluids, or plain water or other cool non-alcoholic beverages. If symptoms are severe or if the victim is known to have high blood pressure or heart problems, treat it as a medical emergency and seek professional attention.

Hypothermia and frostbite

Hypothermia – a drop in body temperature below 35°C (95°F) – is life threatening. While this is the result of exposure to cold, it is most common at temperatures above freezing and in wet, windy conditions. In the early stages, the person will shiver, but as the temperature falls, they may not. They will be uncoordinated and may demonstrate mental confusion, slurred speech and irrational behavior. Merely bringing the patient into a warm environment will not reverse severe cases. Remove any wet or constricting clothing. Place the patient in a pre-warmed bed or sleeping bag and add bottles of warm (*not* hot) water around the torso. If warm water is not available, use one or more warm dry rescuers in the sleeping bag or bed to provide heat. If the patient is sufficiently conscious to protect their airway, give warm (37–46°C or 100–115°F) sweet fluids such as lemonade. Do *not* give coffee, tea, other stimulants or any form of alcohol.

Frostbitten tissue will feel cold to your touch and either numb or painful to the patient. In extreme cases, the tissue will turn white and harden. Do not attempt to thaw frozen tissue until you can ensure it will not be immediately refrozen. It is better to wait a few hours than to refreeze previously frozen tissue. To treat, gently warm the affected areas in a heated space, using lukewarm water where it is possible to immerse the affected area. Rewarming that is too rapid will cause circulatory problems and possibly worsen the tissue damage. Give the patient warm fluids and be alert to signs of shock. If the tissue blisters, avoid breaking the blisters and cover the affected areas with a dry gauze bandage. Prevent injured fingers, toes, etc. from rubbing against each other by placing gauze pads between them. Seek medical attention for all but mild cases, as there is a risk of septicemia and gangrene in more severe cases.

Animal, snake and insect bites and stings

The immediate danger from an animal bite is generally bleeding (see above). However, animal bites can also transmit dangerous diseases, notably rabies and tetanus. These are both life-threatening. Consult a physician or other qualified medical professional after any animal bite. If at all possible, the animal that bit you should be trapped or killed, since tests on the animal may help determine whether or not you need further treatment.

If not treated promptly, the bites of poisonous snakes can lead to serious illness or death. Although only approximately 15 per cent of people struck by poisonous snakes are actually injected with poisonous venom, it is best to assume that the snake has 'succeeded' in its bite until shown otherwise. Even bites from non-poisonous snakes can carry tetanus and require medical attention.

There are two major groups of poisonous snakes. Bites from the pit vipers – including rattlesnakes, copperheads, water moccasins, bushmasters, fer-de-lance and Malayan pit vipers – are characterized by severe burning pain, discoloration and swelling around the fang marks within a few minutes of the bite. The initial reaction is followed by blisters and numbness in the affected area, weakness, rapid pulse, nausea, shortness of breath, vomiting and shock. If 30 minutes after the bite only minimal swelling has occurred, the bite will almost certainly have been from a non-poisonous snake or from a poisonous snake that failed to inject its venom.

With bites from the second group of snakes, which includes coral snakes, cobras, kraits and mambas, initial pain and swelling is minimal, which may fool you into thinking that the bite is not serious. One to seven hours later, however, blurred vision, drooping eyelids, slurred speech, drowsiness, increased salivation, sweating, nausea and vomiting, shock, respiratory difficulty, paralysis, convulsions and coma may develop.

Regardless of the type of snake, get the snake away from the person who has been bitten. If possible, try to identify it or kill it, since medical treatment is different for each type of venom and depends on the doctor knowing what kind of snake bit the victim. Get the victim to a medical facility as quickly as possible, with minimum movement on the victim's part. Immobilize the affected limb, ideally with a splint. Until medical assistance has been obtained, keep the victim comfortable and reassure them. If you are yourself the victim and you are alone, go to a medical facility immediately. Do not wait for someone to find you. Do not give food or fluids or alcohol or stimulants such as coffee or tea. Do not allow the victim to smoke. Do *not* attempt to cut open the wound or suck out the venom. If venom enters through a wound in your mouth, you could lose consciousness or die very rapidly. The next steps are aimed at stopping the venom from moving toward the heart and entering the general circulation.

1   If the victim has been bitten on an extremity, *do not* elevate the limb; keep it level with the body.

2   Place two constricting bands, 2–4 cm wide – for example, a narrow gauze bandage or a rolled up handkerchief – one or two finger breadths above and one or two finger breadths below the bite. If only one band is available, place it on the side between the bite and the victim's heart. If the bite is on the hand or foot, place it above the wrist or ankle. Tighten the band enough to stop the flow of blood near the skin but not so much as to stop the flow of blood to the limb altogether – this is not a tourniquet. You should be able to slide a finger under it. If swelling is present, place the bands on the unswollen area at the edge of the swelling. If the swelling spreads, move the band to keep it above the swelling.

3   If possible, place an ice bag over the area of the bite, but do not put ice directly on the skin or wrap the limb in ice.

4   If the bite is on a limb, use a splint to immobilize the limb. Watch the splint and readjust it if changes in swelling occurs.

Insect and spider bites and stings may cause pain and swelling. The most urgent threat is usually the possibility of an allergic reaction to the stings of bees, wasps and ants, which can lead to shock and death. If there is a stinger present, remove it by scraping the skin with the edge of a knife or with your fingernail. Be careful not to squeeze the sac attached to the stinger, since you can inject more venom by doing so. Wash the area with soap and water. Use ice or cold compresses to slow the absorption of venom, reduce swelling and ease pain.

If there is rapid and severe swelling around the bite, treat it as you would a snake bite. If severe allergic symptoms appear – including difficulty breathing or swallowing, fainting or sudden weakness, increased heart rate, itching, flushing, or generalized reddening of the skin, hives, or swelling of the throat, lips, tongue or eyes, treat it as a medical emergency. Monitor the victim continuously for respiratory and cardiac arrest, initiating CPR if necessary, and transport the victim to a medical facility *immediately*. If you know you are allergic to bee or other insect stings, carry an epinephrine auto-injector and use it. With someone else, check to see if they have an epinephrine kit on them and, if so, use it as instructed on the bottle.

RESOURCE III

Managing stress in humanitarian workers: guidelines for good practice

What follows is a set of draft guidelines for staff support by humanitarian aid agencies, proposed by an expert working group assembled by the Antares Foundation (Amsterdam) and the US Centers for Disease Control (Atlanta). For more information, contact the Antares Foundation, W.G. Plein 269, 1054SE, Amsterdam, The Netherlands (telephone: ++31-(0)20-3308340; e-mail: antares@antaresfoundation.org).

Guiding principle: Managing staff stress is good management practice

Managing stress in staff of humanitarian aid organizations is an essential ingredient in enabling the organization to fulfill its field objectives, as well as necessary to protect the well-being of the individual staff members themselves.

Humanitarian aid work is inherently stressful. While stress can be a source of growth and although many humanitarian aid workers withstand the rigors of their work without adverse effects, many others do not. Both anecdotal reports and empirical studies have abundantly documented the negative emotional consequences of exposure to these stressors on various groups of humanitarian workers. These adverse consequences may include post-traumatic stress syndromes, 'burnout', depression and anxiety, 'over-involvement' or 'over-identification' with beneficiary populations or, conversely, callousness and apathy towards beneficiaries, self destructive behaviors such as drinking and dangerous driving, and interpersonal conflict with co-workers or with family members.

Staff stress and burnout have an adverse impact on the ability of the agency to provide services to those directly impacted. Workers suffering from the effects of stress are likely to be less efficient and less effective in carrying out their assigned tanks. They become poor decision makers and they may behave in ways that place themselves or other members of the team at risk or disrupt the effective functioning of the team. They are more likely to have accidents or to become ill. From the standpoint of the humanitarian aid agency itself, staff stress and burnout may impede recruitment and retention of qualified staff, increase healthcare costs and create legal liabilities.

Humanitarian aid organizations bear a dual responsibility. They must effectively carry out their primary mission and, at the same time, they must protect the well-being of their own employees. The latter role goes beyond a mere duty to shield employees from harm and ensure that they are 'good workers', however. The agency has a positive responsibility, growing out of and consistent with their overall humanitarian mission, to enhance growth and development amongst staff. The agency should be committed to encouraging staff to develop their own skills and knowledge and to enhancing expertise which will increase the likelihood of the agency achieving its field-based objectives.

Although stress is intrinsic to humanitarian aid work, some stress can be prevented or lessened and the effects of stress on individual staff members can be mitigated or responded to by actions undertaken by individual staff members, by managers and supervisors, or by the agency as a whole. The guidelines below are intended to ensure that the agency acts in ways that minimize the risk of adverse consequences for its employees. They are intended to apply to both international and national staff, recognizing that adjustments may be necessary to take into account the unique needs and characteristics of each group.

Principle 1: The agency has a written strategic plan that accepts overall organizational responsibility for reducing the sources of stress, acting to prevent or mitigate the effects of stress, and responding to the unavoidable effects of stress

The plan reflects the agency's understanding of the impact of staff stress on their employees and on the agency's ability to serve their target population, and relates staff support to the overall organizational philosophy. It describes specific policies, programs and practices to create a comprehensive supportive environment for staff. It carries a commitment to examine all aspects of the agency's operations with respect to their effect on managing stress in employees. The plan includes measurable outcome indicators with regard to staff well-being.

A written strategic plan

- The agency has an explicit, written, specific risk assessment for each individual project, including assessment of the overall level of risk, of specific safety and security risks, and of health and mental health (emotional) risks to staff, and develops a specific strategy for risk reduction for that project.

- The agency has written plans for responding to unexpected circumstances – such as forced evacuations or 'critical incidents' – as well as to the normally expected stresses of humanitarian work.

- The agency warns and educates potential workers, both international and national, about the risks of humanitarian work – including the risks of humanitarian aid work in general, the specific risks of the project(s) they will

cont.

continued

be assigned to, and any specific risks they may face as a result of their gender, sexual orientation, race, ethnicity, nationality or other distinguishing individual characteristics.

■ The agency acts to protect staff from and lessen these risks – insofar as it is possible – and it seeks to mitigate those adverse effects that do occur.

■ The agency commits itself to act in ways that reduce the stress on staff that stems from inadequate or dysfunctional organizational policies and practices.
   - It has clear and firm policies forbidding discrimination against staff based on sex, race, nationality or sexual orientation, and forbidding sexual, racial and emotional harassment of any individual or group of staff members.
   - It creates personnel policies that reduce potential organizational and 'bureaucratic' sources of stress and enhance staff resilience.
   - It trains and evaluates managers and team leaders to ensure that they have the requisite competencies to lead teams in complex humanitarian aid environments.
   - It creates an expectation that all staff do their best to develop and use personal stress management skills and creates opportunities and support for staff in doing so.
   - It encourages and provides support for staff in developing their own skills, competencies, expertise and knowledge in ways that will increase the likelihood of the agency achieving its field-based objectives.

■ The agency explicitly recognizes that the needs of national staff and expatriate staff are not identical and tailors its specific policies and programs to respond to the distinct needs of each of these groups.

■ The agency recognizes that office staff and other staff who are in frequent contact with field workers also experience stress, and that the stresses experienced by these groups are not identical to those of field staff. It designs specific policies and programs to respond to the specific needs of each of these separate groups.

■ Agency policies and practices with respect to reducing and mitigating the effects of stress on their employees include mechanisms of accountability to ensure that they are carried out and include mechanisms for ongoing reassessment of policies and practices.

■ The agency recognizes that, in accepting employment and/or an assignment, the employee accepts a commitment to the same goal of stress prevention, mitigation and response as the agency. The agency encourages the individual staff member to hold the agency to its commitment, without fear of reprisal or discrimination and in complementary fashion, in accepting employment the individual accepts a commitment to comply with agency procedures, rules and regulations aimed at reducing stress.

It would be easy to imagine that stress is something that happens to staff in the field solely as a result of their field experiences. In reality, every aspect of an agency's functioning, including hiring and assignment procedures, contract terms, benefits, career development policies and opportunities, procedures for decision making, polices regarding communication and information sharing within the organization, provisions and procedures for supervision and support of field workers, rules and regulations concerning vacations, policies regarding work hours, policies regarding access to communications with home, grievance procedures and the 'culture' of the organization itself, has an impact on the stress experienced by staff.

As a result, stress management is not something that can be separated out from the rest of organizational functioning. It can not be assigned solely to a particular office or individual to manage. It can not be limited to actions the agency takes solely at times of unusual stress. It must, instead, be imbued throughout the organization, taken into account in designing a wide array or organizational practices, and constantly reevaluated. In the same vein, evaluating an employee for the effects of stress is not a one time affair, engaged in after an unusual event or solely at the end of an assignment. Monitoring of stress levels in individuals and acting to prevent or reduce adverse effects of stress is an ongoing process throughout the staff member's time of association with the agency.

Principle 2: The agency systematically screens or assesses the suitability of staff members before hiring and assignment

Assessment is an ongoing process, focusing on factors possibly affecting the likelihood of adverse or maladaptive responses to the stresses of humanitarian work. It begins before a decision is made to hire a staff member, continues throughout the briefing and training period for new staff members, and is renewed whenever an employee is to be offered a new position or a new assignment.

Screening or assessing new and ongoing staff addresses both the risks and stresses of humanitarian aid work in general and the risks and stresses specific to the particular project to which the worker will be assigned, and with respect to factors relevant to creating an effective team. Assessment includes evaluation of:

1 physical and psychological health, past and present

2 influential life events – including past exposure to traumatic events and how they have been dealt with

3 personal characteristics such as resiliency, coping mechanisms and motives for undertaking humanitarian aid work

4 how past difficulties in personal and professional life have been dealt with

5 the staff member's needs with respect to training and or support if they are to carry out their assignment effectively and with minimal adverse effects from the stresses of the assignment.

Assessment of staff suitability

- The agency seeks to develop an evidence-based understanding of the minimum health and mental health requirements for high risk and high stress assignments, based on its own experience and that of similar agencies.

- The agency screens or assesses prospective staff and staff seeking new assignments with respect to factors possibly affecting the likelihood of adverse or maladaptive response to the risks and stresses of humanitarian aid work.

- The agency recognizes that human resources personnel without specific training are unlikely to be effective in carrying out screening or assessment at an acceptable level and consequently uses appropriately educated and trained interviewers for this purpose.

- The agency holds the individual seeking employment or assignment responsible for revealing information that may be relevant to assessing the risks involved in an assignment for that employee and the training and support that they would need to handle it successfully.

In carrying out such assessments, the agency adheres to legal obligations and ethical standards as to what can be asked and what should not be asked. It recognizes, however, that, if performing a job properly requires certain mental or physical characteristics, then inquiry into these characteristics and hiring or assignment decisions based on these standards is generally considered ethically and legally legitimate.

In carrying out such screenings and assessments, the agency recognizes that identifying in an individual's risk factors for adverse responses to expectable stressors of humanitarian aid work is not necessarily a bar to employment but rather a guide to assignment, training, and other means of matching an individual's capacities to the demands to be made upon them.

The agency maintains transparency to the prospective or actual employee with respect to expectations and the nature of their future assignment. Conversely, the individual seeking employment or assignment is responsible for revealing information that may be relevant to assessing the risks involved in an assignment for that employee and the training and support that they would need to handle it successfully. Failure by the individual staff member to disclose such information mitigates the responsibility of the organization but does not release the organization from the responsibility of carrying out a thorough assessment.

Principle 3: The agency ensures that all employees have appropriate pre-employment briefings and training

The briefing/training includes operational orientation, training with respect to safety and security, training with respect to physical (health) self care, training in cultural and political awareness issues related to the area of deployment and training with respect to stress and emotional self care.

Appropriate briefing and training

- The agency ensures that all staff – including office workers and staff who will be in frequent contact with field staff and both national and international staff – receive an adequate pre-deployment briefing and training.

- The agency provides a new briefing and training to ongoing staff when their assignment changes appreciably.

- The agency trains its supervisors and field managers to recognize stress in their subordinates, to engage in team building activities that help mitigate stress in staff, to respond appropriately to stress in their staff and to call for assistance in times of unusual stress.

Training with respect to stress and emotional self care in the field has several elements. In general, it should include the following.

- Education about the expectable stresses of humanitarian work – with as great a specificity as possible with respect to the particular assignment and with respect to risks faced by particular sub-categories of staff.

- Education about the mechanisms of stress response and about how to recognize signs of stress, burnout, critical incident stress and vicarious traumatization in oneself and fellow workers.

- Training in specific stress management techniques and coping skills – for example, relaxation techniques, anger management techniques, self care, the value of sharing experiences with co-workers, the usefulness and limitations/risks of 'defusing' exercises, psychological 'first aid', and the risk of using heavy alcohol consumption as a way of coping.

- Preparation for dealing with the emotional responses of survivors of traumatic events.

- Provision of as much detailed, concrete information about actual conditions in the field as possible. Training in cultural and political awareness issues related to the area of deployment is also helpful.

Understanding of the best ways to respond to stress is a rapidly evolving field. The agency must be committed to a continued process of updating its knowledge and understanding of stress and of procedures for preventing, mitigating or responding to stress, and to incorporating this knowledge in its training programs and support programs.

Although not specifically addressing stress, adequate preparation with respect to operational demands of a position, safety and security, self care (healthcare) and cross-cultural issues that may affect work all reduce stress on the worker. Thus briefing and training should include:

- operational orientation and specific preparation for the operational requirements of the project – including development of skills needed for working with a team

- training with respect to safety and security in the field – including training with regard to risks common to all humanitarian aid assignments and detailed specific information about the risks to be expected in the particular assignment and training in responding to those specific risks

- training with respect to physical (health) self care in the field – including provision of information about pre-deployment immunizations and malaria prophylaxis – and education about self care in the field, such as HIV/AIDS prevention, infectious disease prevention, food and water safety, nutrition, physical exercise, rest and sleep

- training in cultural and political awareness issues related to the area of deployment.

The briefing and training provided should be specifically tailored both to the characteristics of the assignment and the specific needs and characteristics of the individual staff member.

Principle 4: The agency monitors the response to stress of its field staff on an ongoing basis

This can be done through informal observation by supervisors, periodic routine questioning by supervisors, routine administration to staff of self-report questionnaires or periodic informal or formal group stress evaluation sessions.

Monitoring responses to stress

- The agency assesses staff members for signs of stress on a regular, routine basis as well as in the wake of crises. The manager, supervisor or other staff member responsible for such assessment documents that it has been carried out.

- The agency holds individual staff members responsible for reporting signs of stress in themselves and has an explicit written policy of not responding punitively to any such revelations.

Stress is the result of the ongoing, every day pressures of humanitarian aid work – for example, separation from family, physically difficult living and working conditions, long and irregular hours, repeated exposure to danger. It may also result from non-job-related experiences – for example, marital conflict, sickness or death in a staff member's family. Many aid workers develop a façade of toughness and believe that they should not complain. Others may not recognize the signs of stress in themselves. It is the presence of the expectable stressful experiences rather than worker complaints that should trigger agency scrutiny of stress responses in its employees.

The purpose of monitoring stress is to provide a more caring and enabling environment for staff. At the same time, there is a potential for stress evaluation – and subsequent requirements for staff to cooperate with stress reduction programs – to be seen by staff as intrusive or as means to evaluate or control them. To ensure staff participation and cooperation with stress management programs, the agency must explicitly recognize this potential problem and must seek to design policies and procedures that protect staff members from misuse of the process.

Principle 5: The agency provides support, on an ongoing basis, to help its staff deal with the expectable stresses of humanitarian aid work

The agency hold supervisors and field managers responsible – and accountable – for creating a 'culture of responsiveness' around safety, health and mental health issues at the local (project) level. Team building, resolution of intra-team conflict, organizational practices that reduce stress and encouragement of individual staff members' stress management activities are valued and given concrete support.

Protocols for support

■ The agency has written protocols in place regarding ongoing (in the field) training and policies for support of staff with respect to safety and security, physical self care and emotional self care.

■ The agency makes stress assessment and management part of the formal job description of supervisors and field managers.

■ The agency periodically reviews its organizational practices with respect to their impact on staff stress and seeks to identify changes it can make in policies and procedures to lessen the stress on staff that may result from these patterns of organizational functioning.

■ The agency makes clear to employees that it expects them to engage in good practices of self care with respect to their health, to safety and security and to stress reduction.

Psychological support for staff is driven by the understanding that a high level of stressful experiences is inevitable in most humanitarian aid assignments and that, over time, most employees will feel the effects of this chronic stress. Providing such support should be routine and should not be dependent on demands or concerns expressed by the staff members themselves or by observations that an individual is 'under stress'.

The agency should ensure that field managers and supervisors are trained and qualified with respect to knowledge of safety and security practices and procedures; knowledge of practices promoting physical health in the field; knowledge of the potential impact of organizational culture, policies and practices on staff stress; techniques of team building, including facilitating communication and conflict management; ability to recognize signs of stress, burnout, and vicarious traumatization; and skills in stress management and psychological first aid. Field managers should be expected to be role models for staff under their supervision with respect to conducting themselves in ways that mitigate stress – for example, taking appropriate work breaks, carrying out stress reduction procedures such as relaxation exercises. The agency should provide periodic refresher training in these areas for field managers and supervisors.

Much evidence suggests that social supports are the most important protective factor supporting workers in dealing with stress. From a management perspective, team-building and managing of any conflict within the team are very high priorities. The agency also encourages and facilitates unrestricted access to communication between staff members and their families or loved ones.

Many 'bureaucratic' aspects of work management practices can be sources of stress or can provide respite from stress. Although it is common for staff members to use the agency management style as a 'scapegoat', this does not lessen the need to carefully analyze and correct agency practices that may, in fact, augment stress. The agency should have clear, written policies that specify maximum shift time (save in emergencies) maximum work load, time for required rest and recreation and requirements that staff use leave or vacation time. The agency should have a clear written policy that establishes procedures to implement these standards and holds field managers and supervisors accountable for implementing these standards. At the same time, the staff member, too, has an obligation to behave in ways that reduce the likelihood of adverse effects of stress. These include following routine safety and security and health self care guidelines promulgated by the agency, participating in stress reduction activities – such as regulating their own work schedule, taking breaks, taking time off, participating in agency provided stress reduction activities and engaging in personal stress reduction activities.

Principle 6: The agency provides staff with specific support in the wake of critical incidents and other unusual and unexpected sources of stress

The agency should provide psychological first aid, psychoeducation, evaluation and referral to follow up support and care when appropriate. It should have explicit standing plans that ensure it is promptly informed about any extremely traumatic experience that happens to one or more members of an aid team, and is able to respond rapidly.

Specific post-incident support

- The agency provides field managers and supervisors, as well as staff, with explicit guidelines as to the kinds of 'critical incidents' that should be reported to the agency headquarters.

- The agency makes psychosocial staff with specific training in psychological first aid available, on an 'as needed' basis, to consult with staff members after critical incidents or other sources of acute stress in staff.

- The agency has standing arrangements with specialists in such interventions to provide assistance when it is needed.

Sources of extreme stress may include 'critical incidents' such as a serious motor vehicle accident, being kidnapped or taken hostage, experiencing a serious physical assault, being raped, having one's life threatened, or witnessing horrendous events happening to others – including other team members. Other sources of unusual stress may include emergency evacuations, other unplanned terminations of assignments, or personally traumatic events – for example, acute family crises such as an unexpected death in the family.

Experiencing or witnessing such events very commonly – though not universally – causes distressing responses in those who experience them. These responses include, but are not limited to 'post-traumatic stress disorder', 'acute stress disorder', depression, anxiety, pathological grief reactions, destructive or self destructive behaviors, somatic complaints and difficulties in interpersonal functioning – for example, within the team. Even in the absence of direct exposure to horrific experiences, repeated exposure to accounts of the gruesome or terrifying experiences of others – for example, aid recipients – may cause 'secondary' or 'vicarious' traumatization.

Responses may be evident in the immediate wake of a critical event or only after some delay, and may vary in form and degree. They may affect all staff who experience them or only some staff. However, the 'culture' of humanitarian aid work often leads to aid workers denying or minimizing the distress they are experiencing or resisting efforts at providing them support. The response of the agency should be contingent on the occurrence of the event, not the expressed distress of team members.

Helping others deal with traumatic stress, whether due to direct exposure to traumatic events or due to 'secondary' exposure, requires specific training. Neither field managers nor psychosocial workers normally have such training. The agency should employ or contract with specialists in such interventions to provide assistance when it is needed.

Principle 7: The agency provides all staff members with both a personal stress assessment and review and an operational debriefing at the end of their assignment or at the end of their contract

The stress assessment and review is not carried out by human resource management personnel who may play a role in determining the future of the staff member within the organization.

Post-assignment debriefing

- The agency requires that all staff, both international and national, receive an exit personal stress assessment and review, conducted by someone not associated with human resources management, when they end their service on a project – or, in the case of long-term staff, on an annual basis.

- The agency agrees that the staff member's confidentiality is maintained with respect to stress assessments and reviews.

A personal stress assessment and review focuses on how the worker has responded to the stresses they experienced during their period of service. It may explore what their experiences were, what their thoughts and feelings about these experiences are, and how they are dealing with those thoughts and feelings. It focuses especially on their current emotional state and any needs they may have for ongoing support or other interventions. It includes further education about the impact of stressful experiences on an individual, including the possibility, however unlikely, of late-appearing and/or long-lasting emotional effects of work in the field. It explicitly addresses any need for further interventions to reduce adverse responses to stress. It is not aimed at specific organizational change except insofar as it suggests ways the organization can improve its stress management efforts and its understanding of the expectable stresses of humanitarian aid work.

By contrast, an operational debriefing focuses on what the staff member did during their assignment, what happened to them, what the agency and they personally did well or poorly, and what can be done to enhance agency or individual performance. It includes an attempt to define the individual worker's needs with respect to future training and with respect to concrete needs associated with returning home or accepting a new assignment. Although an operational debriefing is not explicitly concerned with stress management, the experience of feeling listened to about field experience and agency practices and of the agency's demonstration of support for the employee's concrete needs during the re-entry transition can also reduce – or, if done poorly, increase – stress in the individual staff member.

Stress assessments and reviews may be useful ways of evaluating and addressing adverse responses to stress at any time during a worker's service with the agency.

They should be routinely required of employees at the end of an assignment and, for staff on long term assignments, at least once a year. They should not be dependent on the staff member having experienced unusual stresses on the job. They should never consist of a one-off intervention in which the staff member simply ventilates about their feelings. Rather they should focus on evaluating the stress level experienced by the worker as a result of their work and on designing appropriate follow-up interventions if needed.

In a stress assessment and review, an employee is asked to be open about personal feelings about their work. This can only be done in an atmosphere of confidentiality, in which the employee feels assured that their reactions will not affect their possible ongoing employment by the agency. For this reason, they should always be conducted by someone who is not part of human resources management, although they may be carried out by someone in the regular employ of the agency. In any case, the person conducting the stress assessment should have training in carrying out such reviews. This is not a matter of concern with respect to the operational debriefing.

Principle 8: The agency provides both practical and emotional support for staff at the end of an assignment or contract

The agency helps staff members prepare for their return home or transfer to a new assignment. Especially in cases of unexpected termination of a project – for example, emergency evacuation – the agency helps the staff member deal with the logistics of relocation as well as the potential emotional consequences.

Practical post-assignment support

- The agency has standing arrangements to make psychosocial staff with specific training in psychological first aid available to consult with staff members in the wake of an evacuation or other premature or unexpected termination of a project or contract.

- The agency has an explicit commitment to provide support to help employees make necessary practical arrangements associated with relocation after an evacuation or other premature or otherwise unexpected termination.

- The agency has a program for assisting staff who are completing an assignment or contract to prepare for the stresses involved in leaving a project and returning home – or taking on another assignment or contract.

- The agency systematically follows up staff with respect to ongoing adjustment or emotional or family problems several weeks after the end of their assignment or contract, or after their return home, and provides services or referrals to services if needed.

cont.

continued

- The agency provides an opportunity, at the end of a project, for office and other support and supervisory staff to be involved in evaluating the project, including exploring lessons learned and feelings aroused.

- The agency provides adequate notice to staff members in the event that a project or the staff member's employment with a project will be terminated other than for emergency reasons.

- The agency eliminates any conditions of service/contract that financially penalize or otherwise negatively impact employees who leave on their own imitative.

It is easy to recognize the stresses of humanitarian aid work itself. The stresses associated with ending service and or returning home are more subtle, but can nevertheless be problematic. They include the pain of saying goodbye to people you have worked with closely, the concrete tasks associated with relocation, and the practical, interpersonal and cultural difficulties in readjusting to life 'back home' or in a new assignment or new job.

Survival in the field depends, both practically and emotionally, on building strong emotional connections to other team members, to others in the aid community and, often, to recipients. No matter what the intentions of 'staying in touch,' the worker has to say what may be final goodbyes and grieve the loss or transformation of intense relationships. Staff should be encouraged to spend time with those they were close to before leaving.

After an unplanned ending it is usually helpful for staff members who will not be returning to the site of their previous assignment to be asked to spend a few transitional days in a 'neutral' place, where they can think and reflect and plan, rather than abruptly returning 'home' or moving on to a new assignment. Unplanned endings also dramatically increase the stress of dealing with practicalities, such as transferring belongings back home. The agency should provide assistance with respect to such needs.

Ending an assignment, whether in a planned or unplanned way, involves myriad practical tasks, many of which may be stressful. They may include finding a new housing, finding a new job or identifying a new assignment, dealing with professional issues such as updating credentials and licenses, dealing with health issues and insurance, and dealing with 'reverse culture shock'. Employees should be encouraged and provided with assistance in developing a 're-entry plan' – for example, explicit plans for returning to work and for following up on medical or psychological needs. Some of the most difficult, yet unexpected stresses may occur when a staff member who has been separated from his or her family returns home. While the staff member is on assignment, he or she is likely to have changed and grown. Family and friends back home may have changed and grown, as well. Children will be older and the experiences and memories of family members and friends have diverged from those of the returned staff member. Support networks from the past may have weakened with the passage of time. The expectations of a returned staff member and their family members may be out of synchrony. Staff should be provided with information about issues that may emerge when they are reunited with their family, as a result of the divergence of their experience and that of their family during their time in the field. Family members of staff should be offered general information about what to expect when a family member returns after a prolonged assignment. Many difficulties, whether practical (for example, difficulties finding a new position), interpersonal (for example, marital conflict), or psychological (for example, delayed grief reactions, difficulty readjusting to the home culture or delayed post-traumatic reactions), may emerge over the course of several weeks or months following the end of a staff member's assignment or contract. Follow up by the agency, with offers of services or referrals to services if required, and development of peer support networks may reduce the resulting stress.

The ending of a project creates strong feelings in office and support staff and others in the agency who have had regular contact with the project, as well. They, too, need an opportunity to be involved in evaluating the project, including exploring lessons learned and feelings aroused.

Principle 9: The agency has clear written policies with respect to the ongoing support they will provide to staff members who have been adversely impacted by exposure to stress and trauma through their work

While laws in effect in many countries may provide a minimal level of protection or support for disabled workers, the agency itself evaluates what support it owes its staff.

Written policies on ongoing support

- The agency has a clear policy against dismissal of employees who have job stress-related disabilities such as 'burnout', depression, or PTSD.

- The agency has policies addressing issues such as continuation of salary and benefits and provision (or financing) of medical and/or psychological services for employees who are unable to continue working for the agency due to job-related stress or injury.

Humanitarian aid agencies' activities place their workers at significant risk of physical injury or adverse psychological effects. On occasion, these may make continued work in the field problematic. National laws vary in the requirements they place on employers in such circumstances and in the practical supports – for example, income, healthcare – provided by the government itself.

Regardless of national law, humanitarian aid agencies make all efforts to ensure that staff members who are physically or psychologically disabled as a result of their work for the agency can continue in employment. This may require assigning the staff member to a position in which they are less exposed to significant stress or trauma, for whatever time is required for recovery.

Humanitarian aid agencies' duty to provide humanitarian aid to those in need extends to their own workers. In some cases, the extent of disability may make it impossible to offer ongoing employment. Agencies may provide disability insurance coverage to fill in gaps in governmental programs of support and insist that health insurance coverage for their staff includes adequate coverage for mental health services and includes provisions for the employee to maintain coverage if they are no longer employed by the agency.

Because of the many different national laws applying to agency staffing in various countries, the agency gives especially careful attention to the impact of these issues with regard to national staff.

RESOURCE IV
Relaxation exercises: sample scripts

A guided relaxation exercise

The following is a script for a relaxation exercise combining breathing and muscle relaxation. Have someone read it to you – or listen to a tape of yourself reading it – in a calm, slow voice, allowing time for you to take and hold breaths, to let out your breath slowly, and to first tighten, then relax your muscles slowly as indicated in the script. After you have done this several times, you will be able to do the exercise without the tape or the reading.

Close your eyes and put yourself in a comfortable position. If you need to, you can make adjustments now or as we go along. Quiet moves will not disturb your relaxation.

Help your body begin to relax by taking some slow, deep breaths. Take a deep breath now. Hold your breath and count silently to three, or five, or ten. Take the amount of time holding your breath that feels good to you. Then let your breath out in an easy, soothing way. Breathe in again and hold it a few seconds . . . and, when you are ready, let it out again. As you let your breath out, imagine breathing out the tension in your body, out through your nose and mouth, breathing out the tension as you breathe out. Do it yet again, breathing in slowly . . . holding it . . . and out.

I am now going to teach you an easy method of relaxation. *Make a tight fist with both hands . . . very tight . . . so tight you can feel the tension in your forearms. Now, let go suddenly . . . Notice the feeling of relaxation flowing up your arms . . . Make a fist with both hands again . . . and suddenly let go. Again, notice the feeling of relaxation in your arms . . . Let your mind move this feeling of muscle relaxation up your arms . . . through your shoulders . . . into your chest . . . into your stomach . . . into your hips. Continue to focus on this feeling of relaxation, moving it into your upper legs . . . through your knees . . . into your lower legs . . . your ankles and feet . . . Now let this feeling of comfortable relaxation move from your shoulders into your neck . . . into your jaw and forehead and scalp . . . Take a deep breath, and as you exhale, you can become even more deeply relaxed . . . You can deepen your relaxation by practicing this again. [*Go back to the place above marked by the asterisk (*) and repeat this section a second time.*]

However you feel right now is just fine. As you become even more relaxed and comfortable, each time you breath out you can continue to drift even deeper into a state of comfort . . . safe and serene . . . When you relax, as you are now, you can think more clearly or simply allow yourself to enjoy feelings of comfort, serenity and quiet. As a result of this relaxation, you can look forward to feeling more alert and energetic later on . . . You can enjoy a greater feeling of personal confidence and control over how you feel, how you think and what you believe. You can feel more calm, more comfortable, more at ease, and more in control of what's important to you.

When you're ready, you can open your eyes, You can feel alert, or calm or have whatever feelings are meaningful to you at this time. As you open your eyes, you may want to stretch and flex gently, as though you are waking from a wonderful nap.

A guided visualization exercise

What follows is intended purely as an example. Visualization exercises are based on identifying a setting that you find safe and relaxing. It may be a particular place to sit in a forest, a walk by the ocean, watching the sun set and the night come on from in front of your house or some other scene. What is important is that you identify a place where you feel safe and relaxed. In the example below, it is walking on a path through the woods, but if this is not a place of safety for you, choose a different scene. Have someone read it to you – or listen to a tape of yourself reading it – in a calm, slow voice. After you have done this several times, you will be able to do the exercise without the tape or the reading.

Put yourself in a comfortable position. Close your eyes. Check whether or not your body feels well supported and ready to become more comfortable. You can help your body begin to relax by taking in an easy deep breath, holding it for a few moments and then exhaling in a soothing, calming manner. Take in a deep breath now. Hold your breath and count silently to three, or five, or ten. Take the amount of time holding your breath that feels good to you. Then let your breath out in an easy, soothing exhalation. Breathe in again and hold it a few seconds . . . and, when you are ready, let it out again. As you let your breath out, imagine the tension in your body being breathed out with your breath, out through your nose and mouth, breathing out the tension as you breathe out. Do it yet again, breathing in slowly . . . holding it . . . and out.

Now you can go to your safe place. Imagine yourself going to the woods that you love . . . You walk slowly across a field, toward the line of trees . . . As you get closer, you can hear the wind rustling in the leaves. You see the green leaves against the blue sky, and you can see the tops of the trees swaying in an ever-changing pattern as the breeze moves them . . . You come to the edge of the woods. As you enter the woods, the air gets cooler, and the fragrance of the leaves on the forest floor greets you. Along the path, the light is bright in some places, dappled in others . . . The air is fresh and the breeze cools your arms and face. The leaves rustle under your feet. The smell and the sounds and the leaves rustling make you feel happy and comfortable . . . At the side of the path, a patch of green moss looks soft and cool . . . You stop for a moment and concentrate on the songs of the birds and the sounds of small animals scampering through the leaves . . . In the distance, a dove coos . . . As you walk, you feel more and more relaxed and comfortable . . . You see a small stream, the water meandering slowly, a leaf floating slowly down the stream. Beside the stream is a patch of soft grass, and you sit on the grass, watching the leaf float down the stream, hearing the water gurgling over the pebbles. The sun flashes on the water, making jewel-like sparkles. You listen to the breeze in the leaves, the birds singing, the water gurgling . . . As you sit and watch the sparkling water and listen to the gentle sounds of the birds and the leaves in the breeze and breathe the cool fresh air, your body becomes more and more relaxed.

Now you stand up and slowly stretch, stretching every muscle of your body . . . and slowly, slowly, you retrace your path. You walk along the path, searching with your eyes for small flowers in the underbrush, recognizing a familiar bush. You pass the mossy bank and soon, the edge of the forest nears. As you leave the forest, the sun shines brightly, warming your skin, and you feel safe and rested and relaxed.

Three brief relaxation exercises

I

Take two or three deep breaths. Each time, hold your breath for a few seconds, then let it out slowly, concentrating on the feeling of the air leaving your body . . . Now tighten both fists and tighten your forearms and biceps . . . Hold the tension for five or six seconds . . . Now relax the muscles. When you relax the tension, do it suddenly, as if you are turning off a light . . . Concentrate on the feelings of relaxation in your arms for 15 or 20 seconds . . . Now tense the muscles of your face and tense your jaw . . . Hold it for five or six seconds . . . now relax and concentrate on the relaxation for fifteen or twenty seconds . . . Now arch your back and press out your stomach as you take a deep breath . . . Hold it . . . and relax . . . Now tense your thighs and calves and buttocks . . . Hold . . . and now relax. Concentrate on the feelings of relaxation throughout your body, breathing slowly and deeply.

II

Stop. Smile to yourself. Relax your jaw and let your lips part slightly. Breathe slowly and deeply. Breathe in, hold your breath for a second or two, then breathe out. Every time you breathe out, say 'relax'. As you do so, try to imagine the tension inside you being breathed out in your breath. Repeat for four or five breaths – even once can steady your nerves and refocus your attention.

III

Press your thumbs and forefingers together. Take a deep slow breath and hold it for two or three seconds. Then slowly release your breath while simultaneously relaxing the pressure of your fingers. Concentrate on the feelings of relaxation your fingers and slowly say to yourself, 'relax'.

References and additional resources

Internationally accepted standards for humanitarian aid organizations

Management of non-profit organizations

Ethical dilemmas of humanitarian work

Health insurance for travelers

Safety and security

Healthcare

First Aid

Managing stress in the field

Working with traumatized people

Internationally accepted standards for humanitarian aid organizations

Codes of good practices and standards of behavior humanitarian agencies should follow with respect to their staff include:

'Recommendations for an Accountable Organization' prepared by the Humanitarian Accountability Project, http://www.hapinternational.org

'Private Voluntary Organization Standards' prepared by InterAction, http://www.interaction.org/ pvostandards/

'Code of good practice in the management and support of aid personnel' prepared by People in Aid, http://www.peopleinaid.org/code/index.htm

'Guidelines for Staff Care,' Antares Foundation, http://www.anataresfoundation.org (See also above, pp. 142–156).

Codes of good practices and standards of behavior humanitarian agencies and their staff should follow with respect to recipients of services include:

'Code of Conduct', International Federation of Red Cross and Red Crescent Societies, http://www.ifrc.org/publicat/conduct/index.asp

'Humanitarian Charter' and 'Minimum Standards in Disaster Response', Sphere Project, http://www.sphereproject.org/ handbook/

'Private Voluntary Organization Standards (Section 7),' InterAction, http://www.interaction.org/ pvostandards/

Management of non-profit organizations

Two books that provide a broad view of issues in managing NGOs are:

Edwards, M. and Fowler, A. (Eds) (2002) *The Earthscan Reader on NGO Management*, Earthscan, London.

Lewis, D. (2001) *The Management of Non-Governmental Development Organizations: An Introduction*, Routledge, London.

A much more hands-on approach, with sections on topics such as personnel policy, budgeting and financial management and fund raising, can be found in:

Wolf, T. (1999) *Managing a Nonprofit Organization in the Twenty-First Century*, Fireside, New York.

Guides to additional resources on NGO management can be found at:

http://www.ngomanager.org/

http://www.reliefweb.int/w/rwb.nsf

Guides to courses – brief and extended – on NGO management can be found at:

http://www.ngomanager.org/

http://www.reliefweb.int/w/rwt.nsf/

Ethical dilemmas of humanitarian work

Terry, F. (2002) *Condemned to Repeat? The Paradox of Humanitarian Action*, Cornell University Press, Ithaca, NY.

Rieff, D. (2002) *A bed for the night: Humanitarianism in crisis*, Simon and Schuster, New York.

Humanitarian Studies Unit, European Commission Humanitarian Office. (2001) *Reflections on humanitarian action: Principles, ethics, and contradictions*, Pluto Press, London.

Health insurance for travelers

For internet sources of information about travel insurance, see:

http://insuremytrip.com/?linkid=13027

http://www.independenttraveler.com/resources/article.cfm?AID=48&category=8

http://www.pactworld.org

http://www.spibrokers.com

Safety and Security

You may be able to find current information about security conditions in particular regions on the internet at one of the following sites:

The Center for International Disaster Information (http://www.cidi.org/sitreps.htm)

The Aid Workers' Network (http://aidworker.net)

The Overseas Development Institute Humanitarian Practice Network (http://www.odihpn.org)

Relief Web (http://www.reliefweb.int/w/rwb.nsf)

InterAction (http://www.interaction.org)

The Expat Exchange (http://www.expatexchange.com/index.cfm).

Doing an internet search under keywords 'safety' and 'security' and '[name of country]' (for example, 'safety and security in Rwanda') may turn up additional sources.

Detailed guidebooks on safety and security for field worker include:

Cutts, M. and Dingle, A. (1995) *Safety first: Protecting NGO employees who work in areas of conflict.* Save the Children, London.

Davis, J. and Lambert, R. (2002) *Engineering in Emergencies: A practical guide for relief workers*, ITDG Publishing and RedR-Engineers for Disaster Relief, London.

Roberts, D.L. (1999) *Staying alive*, International Committee of the Red Cross, Geneva.

Rogers, C. and Sytsma, B. (1999) *World Vision security manual*, World Vision, Geneva.

Security in the Field, United Nations, available online at: http://www.unep.org/restrict/security/security.doc

Operational Security Management in Violent Environments, Humanitarian Practice Network, available online at http://www.odihpn.org/publistgpr8.asp

Useful material on safety of national staff of international organizations can be found in a report prepared for InterAction, *The Security of National Staff: Towards Good Practices*. This can be found online at: http://www.interaction.org/files. cgi/531_sec_nationals_staff_final_doc.doc. The US Peace Corps *Rape Response Handbook* contains a wealth of useful information on rape. It can be found, in adapted form, online at: http://www.lmu.edu/globaled/peacecorps/rape.html

Healthcare

Two good sources of additional information are:

Lankester, T. (1999), *The traveller's good health guide: A guide for backpackers, travelers, volunteers and overseas workers*, Sheldon Press, London.

Werner, D., Maxwell, J. and Thurman, C. (2002) *Where There Is No Doctor: A village health care handbook*, Hesperian Foundation, Berkeley, CA.

Useful current information on health risks in particular countries or regions can be found on the following websites:

The US Center for Disease Control (http://www.cdc.gov/travel/)

The UK Department of Health (http://www.doh.gov.uk/traveladvice/)

The World Health Organization (http://www.who.int/country/en/).

First Aid

Many first aid manuals are readily available in book stores. Two good ones are:

The American Red Cross and Handal, K.A. (1992) *The American Red Cross First Aid and Safety Handbook*, Little, Brown and Co., New York.

The St. John Ambulance, *St. John Ambulance Guide to First Aid and CPR*, Random House of Canada, Toronto.

Online manuals can be found at (addresses are case sensitive):

http://www.parasolemt.com.au/Manual/afa.asp

http://www.vnh.org/FirstAidForSoldiers/fm2111.html

The Blood Care Foundation (http://www.bloodcare.org.uk) claims to get safe blood to almost any location in the world within 24 hours.

Managing stress in the field

A wealth of ideas on managing stress in humanitarian workers, aimed at individual staff members, managers and workers' families, can be found at: http:/www.psychosocial.org

The site includes links to other resources (internet and print), tools for measuring stress and reducing stress, chat rooms and databases of consultants and people providing counselling and support services.

A CD-ROM based course on managing stress in humanitarian workers (in English; Spanish and French versions forthcoming) is available from the Centre for Humanitarian Psychology: http://www.humanitarian-psy.org

Commercial relaxation tapes are available at many bookstores. You can also purchase them over the internet at BarnesandNoble.com or Amazon.com (or search for other sources under 'relaxation tapes'). At the time of this writing, audio clips of relaxation exercises were available at, among other places,

http://www.utexas.edu/student/cmhc/RelaxationTape

http://www.ksu.edu/counseling/csweb/biofedbk/bfsample.html

http://visitors.bestofhealth.com/

http://www.allaboutdepression.com/relax/

If these can not be found, search the internet under 'relaxation exercises audio'. Books addressing the issue of managing stress for humanitarian workers include:

Danielli, Y. (2002) *Sharing the front lines and the back hills: Peacekeepers, humanitarian aid workers, and the media in the midst of crisis.* Baywood Publishing Company, Amityville, NY.

DeWolfe, D.J. (2000) *Training manual for disaster mental health workers*, Center for Mental Health Services, Rockville, MD.

Fawcett, J. (Ed.) (2003) *Stress and Trauma Handbook*, World Vision International, Monrovia, CA.

Figley, C. R. (Ed.) (2002) *Treating compassion fatigue.* Brunner-Routledge. New York and London.

Friedman, M.J., Warfe, P.G. and Mwiti, G.K. (2003) 'UN peacekeepers and civilian field personnel'. In Green, B.L., Freidman, M.J., deJong, J.T.V.M., Solomon, S.D., Keane, T.M., Fairbank, J.A., Donelan, B. and Frey-Wouters, E. (2003) *Trauma interventions in war and peace: Prevention, Practice, and Policy.* Kluwer Academic/Plenum Publishers,New York, pp. 323–348.

US Peace Corps *Team Building Workbook* available online in adapted form at http://www.lmu.edu/globaled/peacecorps/team.html

US Peace Corps *Crisis Management Handbook* available online in adapted form at http://www.lmu.edu/globaled/peacecorps/crisis_h.html

An interactive CD-ROM-based training program in stress management for humanitarian workers, 'Psychological First Aid in insecure environments', is available in several different languages from the Centre for Humanitarian Psychology in Geneva. For more information, see their website www.humanitarian-psy.org.

For a more detailed discussion of the role of humanitarian agencies in reducing stress in their staff, see

Ehrenreich, J. (2005) 'Managing stress in humanitarian aid workers: the role of the organization.' In Reyes, G. and Jacobs, G. (Eds) *Handbook of disaster psychology*, Greenwood/Praeger, Wilton CT.

Working with traumatized people

Bryce, C.P. (2001) *Stress management in disasters*, Pan American Health Organization, Washington, DC. Also available online at: http://www.reliefweb.int/ w/rwt.nsf/d71d40c25ba39cdac1256de8002fe866/2ad91416f2947254c1256e08004b d3fe/$FILE/paho-stress.pdf

Ehrenreich, J.H. (2001) *Coping with disaster: A guidebook to psychosocial intervention*. Center for Psychology and Society, Old Westbury, NY. Also available online at http://oldwestbury.edu/psychology/index.cfm

Enarson, E. and Morrow, B.H. (Eds) (1996) *The gendered terrain of disaster through women's eyes*, Greenwood Publishing Company Westport, CT.

Green, B.L., Freidman, M.J., deJong, J.T.V.M., Solomon, S.D., Keane, T.M., Fairbank, J.A., Donelan, B. and Frey-Wouters, E. (2003). *Trauma interventions in war and peace: Prevention, Practice, and Policy*, Kluwer Academic/Plenum Publishers, New York.

Hodgkinson, P.E. and Stewart, M. (1998) *Coping with catastrophe: A handbook of post-disaster psychosocial after care*. Routledge, London.

Marsella, A.J., Friedman, M.J., Gerrity, E.T. and Scurfield, R.M. (1996) *Ethnocultural aspects of posttraumatic stress disorder*, American Psychological Association, Washington, DC.

World Health Organization (1996) *Mental Health of Refugees*, World Health Organization, Geneva.

Internet resources, with links to many other sites, include:

National Center for Post Traumatic Stress Disorder (http://www.ncptsd.org/)

David Baldwin's Trauma Pages (http://www.trauma-pages.com)

Index

Index

Index